DAVE B

YOUR GUIDE TO LIVING

LIFE

OUT LOUD

RIVER

PUBLISHING

River Publishing & Media Ltd
Barham Court
Teston
Maidstone
Kent
ME18 5BZ
United Kingdom

info@river-publishing.co.uk

ISBN 978-1-908393-34-0
Printed in the United Kingdom

CONTENTS

DEDICATION

Jesus Christ, the Giver of this wonderful thing called life.

Thank you, Jesus, for healing me.

FOREWORD

Dave and I first made contact following on from a forum for young leaders I was involved in. I encouraged those gathered to drop me a line if they wanted to, and to share their stories with me. Dave wrote to me and told me some of his background and his remarkable story of God's goodness to him and his family. I was both deeply moved and profoundly encouraged by his testimony and felt God impress upon me that here was a young man with a distinct purpose in His plans.

Since then we have kept in touch. I keep a folder on my computer desktop containing a number of Dave's original worship songs and have shared these with our worship leaders here at Saddleback. Dave has a gift for communicating the life of God in an authentic way through his music. Now he's doing the same in print.

The full version of Dave's journey towards complete healing from a rare and aggressive form of cancer can be found in the book Mud In The Eye. But in this book, Dave shares the lessons of faith that he and his family learnt through that journey. Having been given a second chance at life, Dave has determined to live it for all he is worth, according to God's purposes for him. Years ago, the phrase Carpe Diem — Seize the day was popular. I think I prefer Life Out Loud. It captures much better the truth that can live with purpose for the long run.

This is a powerful story that reminds us that we serve a powerful God. I commend to you both Dave's ministry and his inspirational message.

Rick Warren, Founder, Senior Pastor, Saddleback Church

INTRODUCTION

Allow me to start by saying a huge thank you for taking time out of your busy life to read this book. If allowed, I believe this book has the potential to change your life. Okay, a grand and confident statement to make in the opening few lines, I know, but I really do believe it. This book is unique because every chapter is underpinned by a very real and honest life story. It is the story of the loud, aggressive, life-threatening cancer that tried to silence and put to rest the life of a young boy, aged just 16. It is a story that charts life's mountaintop moments and also its deep valley experiences. It is a story that has produced many night time tears, but also proves that joy really does come in the morning. It is a story that does not deny the facts of the diagnosis, but embraces the truth that miracles do still happen today. This is actually my story and my name is Dave.

So what is a *guide to living life out loud* all about? It is about one thing: making the most of the rest of your life. Wherever you are reading these words right now, we already have one thing in common: we're both alive! We are both playing our own individual parts in this amazing thing called life. Life is a gift. Unfortunately this is not the dress rehearsal for it – it's the real thing. This is the thing that scares me – not a fear of life, quite the opposite, but a fear of not living. It has made me think. I imagine myself in my old age, in the last stages of life, within moments of taking my final breath here on planet earth, reminiscing on my journey up until this point. What if the last thought I ever had was, "If only…" If only I had made the most of that opportunity … if only I had mended that broken relationship … if only I had told that person that I loved them … if only I had taken a few more risks and not played my life so safely … if only I had shared my faith more … if only I had turned the volume up in my life and lived it a little louder … if only.

Having faced life and death issues at such a young age I now have a perspective on life that some may not yet have. I hope to show you, through the words and pictures in this book, that this weird and wonderful experience called life is actually really incredible. Maybe as you hold this book you're already feeling a little frustrated because, at this moment, for you life is more of a living nightmare than the adventure I've alluded to. Maybe you've just received a serious diagnosis or some other devastating news and currently life is throwing at you more questions than answers. Maybe you are carrying hurts and disappointments. Maybe you just feel weary and don't have the energy to progress or move forward.

If you fall into any of these categories you have picked up the right book. I don't claim to have all the answers, but I may have the answer that you are searching for. Your situation or perspective may not change overnight but together, little by little, we can start to turn up the volume of your life so that you too can begin to live life out loud. We can both make the decision right now to change what our final thoughts in life will be. You may currently be on course to carry the weight of many "If only's", but you can use this guide to steer in a new direction – a direction that changes your "If only's" into "What a wonderful life."

Our allotted time here on planet earth is so short. Think back to this time last year. It's easy to look back and gasp, wondering where all the time went and why it went so fast. I want to make each moment count; I want to live each day as if it was my last. This passion I have for life – I believe you can have it too.

If any of this introduction has stirred something inside of you or even irritated you in some way, why not take on a new challenge with me? Let's work together through this book to turn up the volume of your life.

Together, lets' live LIFE OUT LOUD.

–Dave.

CHAPTER 1
MEET DAVE

This is the part where we become friends. The reason why we need to be friends before we continue is because, in the coming chapters, we have to establish a few things that can only be established on the basis of friendship. First of all, after reading this chapter, you will know that I am relatively normal. I use the word "relatively" with caution. There is nothing that special about me and I don't consider myself any different to the majority of others reading this book.

Secondly, this book is written with honesty. Some of the thoughts and experiences that are shared throughout it are very personal and still very real to this day. These are thoughts and experiences I can only share with people I can call my friends.

Thirdly, in places this book may offend those who are easily offended – not intentionally, of course, but out of a desire to be genuinely open about subjects that, for many, may be too close to home. I hope though, that because of our new friendship, any offence will be short lived and you'll still love me at the end of it. If you are feeling that a commitment of this nature has come far too suddenly in our newfound relationship, don't worry! You have until the end of this chapter to decide if you would like to pursue this friendship or not.

So, I'll start with my birth and quickly bring you to the place where I reach the age of 16. As the plot-spoiling title of this chapter suggests, my name is Dave. It's not the coolest of names that could have been chosen by my parents, Stuart and Irene, but nevertheless I suppose it is a solid one. I'm trying to picture the scene when my father held me in his arms for the very first time after the long hours of labour endured by Irene. He gazes down into my newly formed face, lifts my tiny body and holds me in the air (very similar to that moment in the Lion King) and says, "We shall name him ... Dave!" Given the choice I would have gone for something like "Wolf", "Jet" or "Zorro". It's funny thinking about it now, since baby names in this day and age are considered un-cool if they are easy to pronounce.

So little baby Dave arrived in this world on the 19th September 1986, weighing 8lb 6oz. I was in a very blessed position to be born into a Christian home. Not only that, but to have a father who is a church Pastor. Stuart, my dad, had it in him to produce two more offspring in addition to myself. The first of which was older brother, Andrew, followed by older sister, Becki. I was the baby in the family by a good 10 years. Stuart and Irene have assured me on many occasions me that I was in fact planned ... anyway, moving on...

Being the baby in the family did come with its benefits. Put quite simply, I was the favourite. As Andrew and Becki were of a similar age, it would usually be the both of them who got into disagreements rather than me. I can remember one incredible moment that took place where I was the sole witness in an argument between Andrew and Becki that took a turn for the worst. Just before I paint the scene, it would be good for you to know a little more about my siblings.

Let me start with Andrew. Andrew was the complete opposite to me. He was the more academic of the two Bell boys. Andrew's recreational time would consist of reading a large novel or carrying out some intense calligraphy work. My extracurricular activities would have included dressing up in my Superman outfit and jumping off our large garden wall. I think you see what I mean. As for Becki, let's just say that at the time, she was a teenage girl who knew very well how to use Andrew's more sensitive nature to her advantage.

Right, back to the story. Andrew and Becki were immersed in a fully-fledged argument that resulted in Andrew giving Becki a small clout to the back of the head. Becki then used her initiative, playing to Andrew's more compassionate nature, by pretending that this sudden blow has caused instantaneous blindness. Andrew, with fist raised high, was now made to feel responsible for inflicting a serious and life-changing disability on his younger sister. One word sums up the privilege of witnessing this historic act ... priceless!

Let's learn a little more about Becki. She has always been one to ask questions. Whatever the subject, she is always keen to know every little detail. What should be a five-minute conversation with Becki has the tendency to last an hour due to her intense interrogation. I am told that this was partially interesting when Becki was given that certain "talk" that most parents have to have with their children once they reach a particular age. I think you know the one I mean – the sex talk. I am told that the amount of questioning that resulted was well above the national average, compared to the chats that both Andrew and me received. What was more disturbing to me was the level of intrigue Becki had for the subject at hand. Part way through the talk my sister made a request to my mother: "Mum, I think it would be good idea if I watched you and Dad do it, so I know what it's all about." Outrageous, but brilliant at the same time. Classic Becki.

Let's jump forward to when I was around 12 years old. It was at this point in time when it became apparent that I had two main passions in life – sport and music. My love of sport probably developed simply because I found it difficult to sit still for longer than five minutes. My passion for music was probably passed down from my Dad. He tells me that he was a Christian rock star back in the day. I think the only part of that statement this is true is that he was definitely a Christian. That's possibly a little harsh – he was part of a successful band called the Advocates who produced many records and played at some very prestigious venues.

Sports-wise, I played soccer for my local team and scored 34 goals in my first season. I also loved playing rugby. It's a very satisfying feeling throwing someone to the ground and inflicting a little pain, all within the confines of "a game". Mum did not like attending my rugby matches for obvious reasons.

But music was by far my greater passion. My musical career

began by learning the drums kindly provided by Santa. How he managed to get them down the chimney, I will never know, but they arrived and, with sticks in hand, I set out to be a drummer. After a few years of drumming I decided to place the sticks back on the shelf and took up the guitar. My Granddad kindly donated his acoustic guitar to get me started. I was pretty certain this "instrument" had been crafted just shortly before the wheel, but it seemed to work fine.

I would sit in front of the TV for hours watching Eric Clapton DVDs whilst strumming my little guitar. A defining moment came when watching the blockbuster hit *Back to the Future*. Remember the part where Michael J Fox picks up the guitar and starts to play *Johnny B Goode*? The determined character that I am would not rest until I was able to play this for myself.

Soon I formed a band with some close friends. The band was named *Anonymous*. It's a terrible name, I know, but it was apparently the best we could all come up with. Eventually *Anonymous* saw the light and decided a name change was in order, so we later became known as *Flint*. A little better but not exactly Coldplay. Flint began to attract a little following within the local scene and even recorded an EP. We even reached the heights of the local village carnival. After the departing of a few band members another name change was inevitable. Flint then became the mighty *Atlas*. We supported the likes of *Delirious?* And, on one occasion, American superstar Little Richard at a big charity event in London. My mum told me that we were the best band in the whole world, so it must have been true.

Let's move forward in time a little more. There were three things to look forward to throughout the year in my personal calendar: Christmas, my birthday and The One Event (formerly Grapevine). It has to be said that Grapevine was the highlight of my year. It was a large, family Bible weekend that took place every year. I even think it was equal to, if not slightly better than Christmas. I'm not suggesting that camping at a Christian festival on an agricultural show ground for five days is on a par with the birth of our Lord Jesus – but it does come pretty close! At the end of each event I would go into a season of mourning, commonly known as "the Grapevine Blues", which historically affected many people, especially me and my friends. Waking up on the Wednesday morning after the final night was the worst day in the year. Life just didn't seem worth living any more. At one point I even had the Samaritans on speed dial, just in case.

Throughout my teenage years it was apparent that I was a bit of a practical joker and on most occasions I would cross the line in one way or another. Youth weekends away would often prove this fact. On one occasion I managed to conceal around ten different alarm clocks in the youth leader's dormitory, all set at fifteen-minute intervals starting at 3.00am. I found this prank really funny. Somehow I don't think she did.

I remember another occasion at a cell group meeting where I may have crossed the line again. As mentioned, I have trouble sitting still for very long. I have to be active or doing something or I tend to lose attentiveness. When it came to the prayer section of the evening I decided to sneak out through the back door for some fresh air. I saw a certain boy's bicycle lying there on the driveway. Me being me, I couldn't just walk past it without causing some sort of disruption to this innocent boy's journey home, so I decided to climb up the side of the house, dragging the bike with me, and put it on top of the roof. I walked home with a grin on my face, wondering just how long it would take him to find his bike. Ingenious! Shortly after arriving home, however, I heard the phone ring. I could hear mum in the background, apologising profusely for the fact her son had gone too far again.

We're nearly up to date with the story. I hope after what you have heard so far we are still friends? Throughout these years the local church played a prominent role in my life. My parents educated and imparted to me the importance of church and church attendance from an early age. When having to make decisions such as playing for my local soccer team on a Sunday morning or going to church, the matter was clear cut and non-negotiable. Sometimes I would question if church was really that important. Surely the odd game of football wasn't much of an issue? But I believe God honoured my decision to put local church first by lining up a team that played the majority of its matches on a Sunday afternoon, meaning that church was always attended.

Okay, now you know all the important stuff about me. It's official – we're friends. Wahoo! At this point I would give you a rather awkward, but warm embrace; maybe even a small kiss.

Our story has brought us from my birth up to the young age of 16. Overall I was very content with life and rarely down. I had great relationships with family and friends and kept church a priority within my life. There was no room in my life for illness, struggle or setback. I could never really entertain such an idea. Like most 16-year-old boys I also thought I was invincible and just presumed, like many, that such things as a serious illness or a major setback would not affect me. After all, I went to church,

I didn't drink, I didn't smoke, I didn't do drugs... What could possibly happen to me?

With Love,

Your new friend, Wolf. Sorry, I mean Dave.

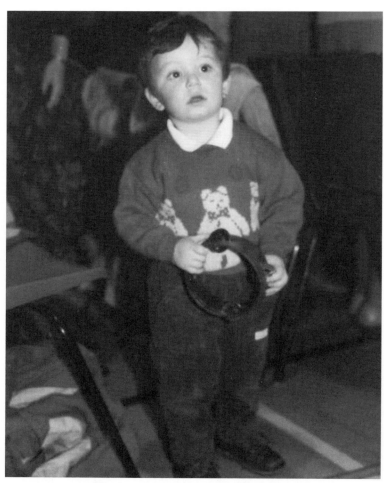

Me at the age of 2. Not too happy with Irene's choice of clothing for me on this particular day. The white bear wearing a bow tie is enough, let alone a small wooden tambourine. Thanks Mum.

CHAPTER 2
WORDS FRAME YOUR WORLD

If we want to live LIFE OUT LOUD we need to understand that the words we speak can frame our world.

Change is one of the only constant things in this life, which means that we all experience it from time to time. But in most people's lifetimes I would imagine that there are very few days like these – the days that represent a crossroads in life, with a signal flashing to say a major change is on the way.

For some of us it is a change of job, maybe a house move or a new car, but for others some change does not feel like it is for the better. Upon approaching these symbolic crossroads in life there is usually no Angel standing on the junction to inform us of what lies a head. It's not usually that simple.

A new chapter of change in our family began one day. It wasn't marked by a new promotion, a house move, or anything positive. In fact, it seemed quite the opposite. Instead of signifying a time of blessing, it seemed that all hell was let loose and sent on a personal assignment to intimidate and cause un-rest for the Bell family. It began with the untimely death of my Grandma, who slowly lost her ability to communicate as Alzheimer's disease took her away little by little. Soon after this my other grandparents were taken from us.

During this strange period my Mum's health started to become an issue. What should have been a fairly routine operation became much more serious. We expected her to be home within a few days, but her blood pressure started to drop and her wound refused to heal. She was taken back to the operating theatre many times and, in the process, picked up a significant infection that took many months to sort out.

A few months later we believed that Mum was back to full health, but this was not quite the case. One morning she tried to get out of bed, but was so overwhelmed with pain that we knew something far more serious was taking place. She has suffered with back pain for many years, but this was certainly on a different scale.

This all happened just before our annual Grapevine celebration. Mum tried to hide the pain, but it was obvious that she could not walk. Since she was determined to make the event in spite of her physical condition, she resigned herself to the fact that she would need to be escorted around the event in a wheelchair. Whilst on site, a guy who happened to be an orthopaedic surgeon examined her on an old wooden chair in the middle of a muddy field. He was so concerned that he made an immediate appointment for a scan.

Within a matter of days Mum was admitted to hospital for

major back surgery, during which bars and screws were fitted. The operation was successful, for which we were all very grateful. As a family we breathed a collective sigh of relief and assumed that the storm in our lives was passing. Soon we would see a break in the overshadowing clouds. In fact, in the distance more clouds were beginning to gather. Ill heath had surely taken its toll on us, but little did we know ... our greatest challenge was still to come.

In February of 2003 I woke up one morning and, following my usual routine, went into the bathroom to brush my teeth. I looked into the mirror and noticed that something was not quite right with my right eye. Not thinking too much of it I set about my day and carried on with my fun-filled life. A few days passed, however, and the problem with my eye continued, so I decided a trip to the doctors was in order.

After a brief examination some drops were prescribed to counteract the possible infection that was probably causing the slight laziness in my right eye. A week later there was still no sign of improvement. My eyelid was beginning to droop and looked completely different to my other eye. Upon hearing this, my local doctor referred me to an ophthalmologist in my home town of Lincoln.

The appointment day arrived and I went to the hospital to see the specialist. He called me into his room and started the procedure of examining my eye. I rested my chin on the device that was able to see into the back of my eye. After a bit of prodding around and a few confused expressions the doctor leant back in his chair and said that there was something going on behind my eye that he didn't like the look of. He didn't say any more, other than his findings were a little out of his area of expertise, so he would be referring me to one of the leading eye surgeons in the country, located around 50 miles outside Lincoln. I left the hospital that day a little upset. What I thought was only a minor infection was obviously proving to become something bigger. I allowed my mind to wander a little too far, thinking of possible outcomes. But surely it couldn't be anything too serious?

Within a week the appointment came through to see my new consultant. We all got into the car and did the 50 mile journey from Lincoln to Leicester. Stuart was behind the wheel so it took a good 40 minutes longer to get there than if I'd been driving, but nevertheless we arrived. Entering the waiting room I noticed that the general demographic of people with eye conditions seemed to be those of around 108 years of age – and then there was 16-year old me. The nurse called me through to check my vision. By this time my eye was completely swollen over and I had to tilt my head right back to see clearly. I did my best to read the little letters on the wall. My left eye was perfect. The right eye not so good. I returned to the waiting area until I was called again.

Next it was the registrar's turn to have a look at me. I went into the room and placed my chin on the familiar machine so that she could have a look into the back of my eye. After an examination in complete silence she got up and left the room immediately without saying a word. I looked over to my Dad at this point and said, "I don't think that is a good sign." Within a matter of minutes the door open again and in walked the senior consultant with the registrar following closely behind. He formally introduced himself and asked permission to carry on with a further examination. The room was in complete silence and I could hear my heart beating louder and faster. He then allowed me to sit back from the machine while he explained some of his findings. He confirmed what the previous doctor had said, highlighting a problem in the orbit of my eye. I was told that as a matter of urgency I must come back to the hospital within three days where I would undergo a serious biopsy on the right orbit of my eye. He shook my hand and left the room, knowing that the next time we would meet would be just before the surgery.

We got back into the car and the atmosphere was a little different to our first journey. In all honesty we shed a few tears – possibly out of frustration, but also confusion. I thought this was just an infection! A few drops, a sore eye and then I will be back to normal. Three days passed very quickly and it was time to get back in the car again to do the 50 mile journey to Leicester. It was on this journey that we learnt our first lesson: Words frame our world. I made a little throw-away comment suggesting that I would be stuck on a ward full of old people and my bed would be conveniently placed between two old men with me right in the middle. We arrived at the hospital and walked onto the ward to find that my little comment in the car was to become a reality.

We came to a ward full of old people and guess what? A spare bed assigned to yours truly was positioned between two very old men who looked clinically dead. As a family we then decided very quickly that our language was going to have to change. We needed to speak positivity into our situation. The Bible tells us that the power of death or life is in the tongue. This situation was neither death nor life at this point, but it was very important to me. From that moment my language changed and I began to speak out what I wanted to see happen.

As I was still young and a little scared of the operation I thought that the best scenario would be for my parents to stay with me overnight in the hospital. I know that this request was a little optimistic, as this is not usually the done thing, but it didn't stop me speaking it out. I cautiously asked the staff nurse if this request might be possible. To my amazement she escorted us to a curtained-off section of the ward, revealing a more private area with three empty beds. An answered prayer. The words we use frame our world.

The light relief quickly passed when my consultant arrived in full surgical attire ready for my operation. I felt a little more comfortable seeing him in a suit. At this point my eye was completely closed. In actual fact, it looked very disturbing. Before the operation my consultant took a number of photographs of my eye that would later be used in study guides for medical students, due to the rare nature of the problem. The time eventually arrived for me to have the operation. My mum accompanied me into the preoperative room where I lay on a bed ready for the anaesthetic.

While she was holding my hand a profound moment took place. In the middle of all the highly qualified medical professionals working around me Mum began to sing. The room calmed, possibly out of respect, or it may well have been the fact that my mother is not known for her vocal abilities, demonstrating this by changing key around 8 times without even noticing! Joking aside, it turned out to be a very special moment that even made me a little tearful. She sang the words from a Delirious? song: "God is bigger than the air I breathe, this world we'll leave. God will save the day and all will say my glorious." My eyes closed and I was in the hands of a skilled surgeon who would begin to make a long incision underneath the line of my eyebrow.

During my time in the recovery room my family were called in to see the consultant. They were taken into a small side room. A room more suitable to deliver difficult news? My parents were then informed that their son had contracted a rare and aggressive disease and that the prognosis at this stage was uncertain. It may be something as "simple" as loosing my right eye. Or worse, depending on what this was, my life might be cut short at the age of 16.

I woke up from the operation to see my Dad's face staring at me. With panic in my voice I said, "Dad, Dad what have they said? Am I going to be okay?" He looked at me with a straight face and said, "Dave, the doctors have seen something that they are not happy with, but whatever this is we are going to fight it with all that we have." I went to sleep that night with the song My Glorious playing in my ears.

The results were going to take around seven days to process, so we left the hospital with a view to come back for the results within the week. I then endured the longest week of my life to date – a week of the unknown; not knowing what was around the corner; not knowing the certainty or the outcome of my future.

Yours truly, attempting to look cool with my signature rock stance. When leading worship nowadays I still use this famous move when prompted by the Holy Spirit. Many people have found salvation when I do this...

—LIFE OUT LOUD GUIDE—

From this chapter we learn that words frame your world. The power of life and death is in the tongue. We need to learn to speak into our future and verbally say what we want to see. *Speaking negatively will attract negativity. Speaking positively will attract positivity.*

THINK: OUT LOUD:

What strikes you about what you have read?

What is your natural response to situations in life?

Do you respond with positive or negative thoughts and words? What impact would thinking and speaking positively have?

READ: OUT LOUD:

Read Proverbs 18:21 MSG:

"Words kill, words give life; they're either poison or fruit— you choose."

PRAY: OUT LOUD:

Father, I want my thinking and speaking to be positive and full of life. I am sorry for the times that I have allowed negativity to be the frame of my world. Today I choose life and I ask that I would see the fruit of your kingdom through the words that I speak, in Jesus' name.

LIVE: OUT LOUD:

Each morning practice thinking and speaking positive words over yourself, your family and your life. See the impact this has on your day.

CHAPTER 3
BAD NEWS

Bad news can often get in the way when we are trying to live LIFE OUT LOUD. So how do we deal with it?

I woke up the next morning and, as usual, went to the bathroom to check my eye. I looked into the mirror with a little faith, hoping to see that my eye had returned to normal and that there would be no need to drive back to the hospital for my results. My eye was still the same if not worse. I got dressed and went downstairs, ready to get in the car for the trip to Leicester. I noticed that, unusually, Dad was wearing his suit. But not thinking too much about his choice of clothing I got into the car. Looking back now, I think Stuart's decision to wear a suit was more profound than I first thought. It made a statement. To me it showed that he was taking charge of this situation and from the very outset we were going to approach it very seriously. It taught me that, even though the news you or I might hear today may well change our lives, we still need to "dress" smart – to be prepared and take it seriously.

The car pulled away from the house and I remember thinking, "When we pull back onto the drive later, what will have changed? What will I be thinking?" We learnt in the previous chapter that words frame our world, so we started the journey with a prayer and asked God to be very real to us and to guide us through the next few hours.

Eventually we arrived at the hospital and made our way to the waiting room. Dad sat next to me in his suit and Mum was on the other side. Few words were exchanged; it was just the sound of heavy breathing and hearts racing. The consultant called my name and led me into a room to have my eye cleaned and examined by one of his team. During this time my parents were taken into a small side room to speak with the consultant before I joined them. I lay on that bed anxiously wondering what was been discussed. Then it was my turn to join my parents in the consultation room.

I sat down in the chair feeling a little faint. I then heard words spoken over me that I never thought I would hear in a lifetime, let alone at the young age of 16. I was told that I had contracted a very rare and aggressive cancer, which meant I was a 1 in 3 million statistic. I gazed over at my parents to see my mum fighting back the tears, not wanting me to see her cry. Dad's complexion was pale, however his suit was still in tact. My consultant informed me that I was now to be passed over to the children's Oncology department who would take me on from here. After a few handshakes and best wishes were done we left the room.

Outside the hospital I phoned my brother and sister to share the news with them. I found it hard to speak to them through the tears and equally difficult to understand them through theirs.

I can see myself getting into the lift with Mum and Dad and pressing the button for the fourth floor. Four floors later the lift doors open and I anxiously step out. I tilt my head right back so that I can see and head towards the sign that says "Ward 27 – Children's Oncology". I go on ahead and open a set of large wooden doors, the entrance to Ward 27. Even as I sit in my office today, recalling these events, I have already had to stop a few times to wipe away a few tears. It still feels very real.

I open the large set of wooden doors and it is as if I have walked through that famous, fictional wardrobe into another world or some other make-believe place. But this is no fairy tale, this is real life. I take a few more nervous steps inside with Mum and Dad by my side. It's like watching one of those news documentaries that we only ever see from the safety of our own, peaceful homes. Lots of little children lying in beds with no hair and feeding tubes coming out of their noses. I can't distinguish between life and death in some sleeping children.

A friendly nurse called Rachel takes me on a brief tour of the ward. She leads me into a room where I find a little bald child sat on the end of his bed. I stare into his eyes, trying to contemplate the fact that I will be "one of them" in a matter of days. I am introduced to a doll that is fitted with a Hickman line. Rachel informs me that I will be fitted with one and this is how they will administer the chemotherapy and also take blood.

We left the hospital that day having received life-changing

news. I suppose out of sheer naivety I thought that cancer treatment would involve taking a few pills, losing some hair and then I would be on my way again. In my situation this would not quite be the case.

One week later I returned to the hospital to be subjected to a whole week of intense testing. Every test you can think of I had done, all in one week. By this time my eye condition was at the worst stage as the tumour was aggressively forcing my eyeball out of the socket. Sorry for being a little graphic, but that's what was happening. Here is the "short" list of what took place during the week of testing:

- A series of blood tests
- Kidney function tests
- MRI Scans
- CAT Scans
- Chest X-Rays
- ECG Heart test and scan
- Hearing Tests
- Full body bone scan
- Visual Tests and photographs taken for doctor's training materials
- A visit to the sperm bank
- Neurology Tests
- Lumber puncture
- Hickman Line surgically fitted under general anaesthetic

Not too bad for a week's work! A few of the procedures listed above are, for obvious reasons, quite hard to weigh up. At 16 you're not expected to have to think too much like an adult, especially when it comes to planning for the future and thinking about the possibility of having a wife and children. I had to change from a boy to a man overnight, instead of waiting until the time came naturally. I was faced with big decisions that would have consequences for my future.

I was told that due to the intense chemotherapy my body would endure it would be highly unlikely that I would be able to have children naturally. Most 16 year olds never contemplate such issues, concerning themselves more with matters such as, "What's for dinner tonight" and "When will it be ready?" I am one of the few who had to grapple with bigger issues than that. I am so grateful for having such an amazing relationship with my Dad, where I feel comfortable talking about most issues with him, especially this one.

It was at this point that I learnt another valuable lesson. In hard times laughter is often the best medicine. I decided that I needed to make light of these awkward situations. Instead of going to the sperm bank all alone, for instance, I thought it would be appropriate to take a few of my pals with me. So Jeff Lucas, the famous Christian speaker and author and my Dad accompanied me on the journey, indulging in some laddish humour (which I won't repeat) along the way, before the proceedings continued. They sat in the waiting room for me while I continued on to "do the necessary".

In my head I had somehow built up a mental image of what would happen. I would be escorted into a candlelit room, scented with cinnamon, with a few "choice" images strategically placed around the wall. But we didn't have private healthcare, so instead I was shoved into a disabled toilet with nothing more than a smile and a plastic cup. A short time later, however, I emerged into the waiting room, sample cup raised high, yelling "Victory!" at the top of my voice. A ripple of applause greeted my return – from Dad and Jeff at least. To be honest, everyone else looked a bit disturbed and traumatised. For me it had been the best test so far! But now onto more serious matters.

My week of intense testing is coming to an end. There is still one more procedure to take place, though, the fitting of the Hickman line. The thought of this keeps me awake for many nights. The idea of a plastic tube being inserted into the top of my heart and coming out of the left hand side of my chest is sickening. I am informed that this might have to stay with me for a year. The time comes and it is my turn to go into theatre. I stop and ask Mum if I can just run away and believe that God will heal me, as I don't think I can face any more. We both cry and Mum tells me that it would be irresponsible for us to do that, but God will be with us. I walk towards the operating theatre with Mum and the nurse guiding me. I am led into the anaesthetic room where I lie on a bed and begin to cry. The anaesthetist tries to find a vein beneath all the bruising of the previous injections. Before he starts to inject the anaesthetic we ask if we can pray. Mum holds my hand and tries to pray as best she can, whilst fighting back her emotions. We pray that Jesus will come into the room with me and hold my hand throughout the operation since Mum will not be there. Following the new tradition, as my eyes begin to close my mum begins to sing the simple chorus, "God is bigger than the air I breathe. God will save the day and all will say, my glorious." I'm not too sure what put me out first, the anaesthetic or Mum's harsh tones. Neither are pleasant experiences.

My eyes gradually open an hour later in the recovery room. I feel a deep pain down my left hand side. As I am wheeled back to the ward I realise that the journey has begun and life is going to change drastically from this point on. I look down at my chest to find a long tube with two ends strapped up with some white tape. I have a brief lesson in all the procedures relating to how the line will be used and what to do in an emergency. The line is so uncomfortable and at first it restricts a lot of movement. Sleeping is difficult and I am constantly nervous of catching it or it splitting. This will be a part of me for a long time to come. I can't see it getting any easier.

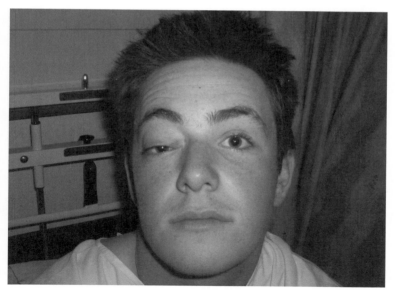

As a family we chose to leave out the really bad pictures of my eye, as they are quite horrific. However, it is important that you at least have a little glimpse of the giant we were facing. This picture was taken just before my eye biopsy. Sorry about the hair.

—LIFE OUT LOUD GUIDE—

When facing adversity we need to take control. Instead of telling God how big our problem is we need to tell our problem how big our God is. We need to be very clear that the negative thing happening to us was never God's intention. It is not some form of punishment for previously committed sin, though if He needs to, God will sometimes permit times of trial so that His work can be displayed in our lives. But God will never take us to a place our character cannot handle. Enjoy the journey and give God the glory.

THINK: OUT LOUD:

What strikes you about what you have read?

How big is your God?

What is your understanding of Him?

Do your problems sometimes eclipse God? How can you change this?

READ: OUT LOUD:

Psalm 121:1-2 NIV:

"I lift up my eyes to the mountains—where does my help come from? My help comes from the LORD, the Maker of heaven and earth."

PRAY: OUT LOUD:

Father, help me to see you as you are. May I never box you in or limit you. Help me to know that you are bigger than any problem I face. You are the great God, the great King. I thank you that no matter what mountain I face, you are there for me as my helper and friend. Help me to live in this truth daily in Jesus' name.

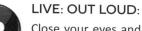

LIVE: OUT LOUD:

Close your eyes and think about God and all the aspects of His character that come to mind. Think about His majestic nature, that He is the King of Kings and Lord of Lords. Think about His creation, His love, His power and strength, His generosity, mercy, grace, peace and what He has done in your life. Allow your understanding of God's bigness to grow and grow. Practice this a couple of times a week

CHAPTER 4
CHANGE

The only constant thing in life is change. The good and the bad. Is it still possible to live LIFE OUT LOUD when everything we know is always subject to change?

Before we start this chapter together I thought it would be good to extend some advice. If you or a close family member is about to start any treatment for cancer, I suggest you skip this chapter. I'm sure you're now wondering what this chapter contains and you may well have the urge to keep reading. But friend to friend, please don't. Right now it's more important that you concentrate on the faith-filled chapters. The mind is a very powerful thing and I don't want your mind to be filled with some of my personal challenges – many of which may not be relevant or helpful to your own situation.

Instead, I'll do a deal with you – once you've come out of the other side of your battle, I give you permission to go back and read this chapter. We can then share our experiences without fear or worry. Who knows, we will maybe even smile thinking about it.

Chemotherapy

Eventually the epic day dawned and my treatment was about to begin. The night previous to this is still vivid in my memory.

I nervously walk up the stairs to my room to go to bed knowing what lies ahead the following morning. Mum and Dad come into my room and sit on the end of my bed. We pray together and then I listen to a healing CD by Tony Miller just before I fall asleep.

This daunting morning has arrived. I am not dreaming, this is my life and today is the day that I start chemotherapy. I pack my bags, my quilt and pillow and get into Dad's car. We start driving and head for Leicester. Little do I know, this journey is going to become very familiar over the next few years. Why have I taken my quilt and pillow? Here's the hard part: each treatment is three days long and the majority of this time is spent lying in a bed. An hour and half later we arrive at the Royal Infirmary. It should have been considerably less, but once again the Reverend was behind the wheel.

I arrive on the ward and am swiftly taken to a little side room where I am going to spend the next three days. I am informed that I will be given three chemotherapy drugs throughout my stay, as follows: Vincristine, Ifosfamide and Actinomycin-D.

My Hickman line is then connected to an IV machine, which pumps a fluid called mesna around my body to help prevent internal bleeding and damage to my major organs. This is injected constantly for the entire three days, meaning that well over six litres of the stuff is passing through my body. Within five seconds of the mesna starting I begin to feel really sick and get a strange metallic taste in my mouth. I start to worry. If this fluid is only there to protect me, what will the actual chemotherapy feel like?

Three hours later it is time for my first lot of treatment. I already feel sick and very weak before it begins. A large black bag is hung up on the machine and then connected to the spare tube on the Hickman line. The only way I can describe it is that it feels as though I am slowly dying. I feel incredibly sick, weak and very pale, as if life is draining out of my body. This is a feeling you wouldn't wish on your worst enemy. I am violently sick a few times during the night. I struggle to move for the next three days. I start to become acquainted with the echo of small helpless children crying out in pain and being sick at regular intervals. I am being monitored and tested vigilantly for the next three days. The only thing I have to look forward to is when my family arrives to visit. Seeing them walk into the room infuses a little hope and encouragement.

Since I was 16 at the time, I had the choice to have my treatment on either the children's ward or the adult ward. The logic behind my choice was very simple: be stuck on a ward full of old people or have a PlayStation 3 at the end of my bed. The PlayStation 3 won. However, there was one other advantage to the children's ward. I was allowed a family member to stay with me through the night. I ruled out Dad straight away because he doesn't really like hospitals. The perfect person was Mum. She was amazing, a young Florence Nightingale. At night time she would sleep near to me on a little fold out bed and we watched DVD's together to try to pass the time. She took all my bottles of wee to be tested throughout the night, cleared up my sick and prayed for me whenever I was feeling low.

The end of my first session is getting closer but it still feels like a lifetime away. Once the final drip of mesna has gone into my body I am allowed to go home. Later this morning Dad arrives to take me home. I walk slowly towards the lift, still feeling very fragile and weak. I open those big double doors again. It is time to leave Neverland or walk back through the wardrobe. My time here is far from over, however. It has only just begun...

Two hours later I arrive home and lay out on the sofa straight away. Lots of thoughts are running through my mind and I am now very conscious that my thinking and way of life is going to change. I just want to reach for the phone to call a few friends and see if they want to play soccer with me, but it would be physically impossible. I'd like someone to call for me and ask if I want to go swimming, but now this Hickman line is in, so I can't. I make a conscious decision that I won't be able to finish this journey by myself or even with the help of friends and family.

Time passes slowly through to the evening and I lie awake on my bed. I listen to Tony Miller's healing CD again and eventually fall asleep. Unfortunately, I wake up many times in the night due to having nightmares. I wake suddenly several times, believing that I have been asleep for hours, but it has only been five minutes. This is caused by the high strength anti-sickness drugs I have to take. The following morning I wake feeling very sick and incredibly weak. It feels like every time I so much as breathe, it hurts. The following Wednesday I drive back to Leicester with Dad for my IV dose of Vincristine.

My treatment protocol states that this will happen on a weekly basis for the first month. Towards the end of the first week of treatment I start to feel very unwell. My temperature reaches 39 degrees and higher, so I am rushed to the local hospital where I have to spend the night. At the end of this week I sit down with my family to tell them that I physically can't do this again. I can't do one more session, let alone another six month's worth. I want the "overnight miracle" so that I don't have to go through this any more.

A week or so later I wake up to find big clumps of hair beside me on my pillow. My hair is beginning to fall out. I call my brother-in-law, Glen, to see if he will come round to shave my head as the bald patches are fast becoming too big to be covered. It quickly becomes a family ceremony and everyone gathers around to see the final strands of hair flutter to the floor. In a matter of days all my hair is totally gone – no eyebrows, no eyelashes. I am so bald you can almost see what I am thinking!

I have many memories of Ward 27, but one of them is still very distinct to this day. I remember lying asleep in my hospital bed and waking to see people walking down the corridor carrying Christmas presents towards a little boy's room. I had met this little boy on my very first visit to the ward. By now he had become a little friend to me and I would often play my guitar to him whilst he sat on the end of my bed playing on his Gameboy. More and more people walked down the corridor holding presents, trying to bring a sense of joy in a very heavy atmosphere.

I made an attempt to get out of bed to try and see what was happening. I stumbled down to his room with my drip following closely behind. I opened the door and his room was filled with Christmas decorations and in the corner stood a large Christmas tree with bright lights and lots of colour. The little boy, very underweight and pale, was softly sleeping in his bed. I asked one of the nurses why they had all the decorations and presents, since it was only the end of November.

She replied in a sombre voice, "The family are doing Christmas early this year, Dave, as he's not going to be around for much longer." A few days later this small child left Neverland, walked back through the wardrobe, never to return to this world. I believe he went to be with Jesus, where he is now free from any disease.

Radiotherapy

My protocol originally stated that if the tumour responded well to the treatment, then radiotherapy would not be needed. However, during my chemotherapy treatment new research identified that radiotherapy was necessary in all circumstances. As you can imagine, to go through all of the above and then be confronted with the certainty of having intense radiotherapy … this news nearly made me give up.

After having a long chat with my consultant, however, where I shared my worries and concerns, she underlined the fact that radiotherapy was going to be a necessity – so that was that.

We eventually get the appointment to see a specialist

consultant in Nottingham who will take me through this unexpected stage of my journey. We get into the car again and make the hour-long journey to Nottingham City Hospital. Dad has his money ready for the car park in the previous county, as he always does. We walk into the waiting room and sit, wondering what the new consultant will be like.

The door opens and I hear my name called. Out walks a man who is vertically challenged and looks like he was born in a laboratory. Dad, Mum and I go into the room and sit down. The consultant's first words are, "Who have you brought with you today then David?" I am very tempted to inject some humour by saying that I have brought my children with me, or something along those lines, but I resist and tell him that they are, in fact and quite obviously, my parents. This initially light atmosphere then makes way for possibly the lowest point of my journey so far. After reading extensive lists of the affects of chemotherapy, I am now presented with a new list of the affects of radiotherapy. They are...

- Cataracts
- Damage to Pituitary Gland
- Possible deformity to the bone structure on the right hand side of my face
- Damage to the tear ducts
- Permanent loss of right eyebrow
- Permanent loss of right eyelashes
- Damage to the surface of the eye
- Damage to the skin surrounding the eye and the rear of my head

Now that's a list for you. Once this has been reported to us, Dad goes rather white and leaves the room for a few minutes. I request to lie down as I feel faint. The consultant now goes on to explain that the Radiotherapy sessions are done daily and I can have up to 25 intense sessions that will take place alongside all my remaining chemotherapy treatments. He also explains that I will have a mask made of my face that will be used to line up where the radiation is fired.

We get into the car and drive back to Lincoln. It's a very quiet journey home and I shed a few tears out of frustration over the situation.

A few days later we make the trip back to Nottingham for the specialists to design and make my mask. I think that this will be a simple procedure, but it turns out to be a very long and awful experience. I am asked to lie down on a surgical table whilst three white-coated people gather around me and get me into position. Two tubes are inserted into my nose and then a hard setting rubber is poured all over my face. I am told to remain totally still for fifteen minutes until the rubber sets. Then plaster is poured on top of the rubber surface.

I obviously can't see anything or even hear anything as the plaster has run into my ears and I am in total darkness. I have to breathe through the two tubes in my nose without moving any part of my face. Eventually the mask begins to set and it takes two of the three staff to pull it away from my head. This procedure is finished and I am now ready for radiotherapy. In the meantime, the consultant had been working on a radiotherapy plan to calculate the correct dosage of radiation and identify an exit point – in other words, how the radiation will leave my body.

Many in our nation remember November 11th for all the soldiers who died in the Second World War. I also remember this day for two other reasons. Firstly, it was the day I started radiotherapy and secondly it was the same day that I passed my driving test. One of our close family friends, Carol, offered to help with a lot of the driving to and from Nottingham for the next month. This worked well as Mum had never driven out of Lincoln before and I wouldn't have to permanently adopt the brace position in the passenger seat!

Once again I get into the car and, once again, drive to a hospital. An hour later we arrive and walk into the waiting room and guess what, the average age is around 108 again, so I feel slightly out of place.

My name is called and it is now time for a whole new experience. I am constantly running the list of possibilities and side effects through my head as I follow the nurse down the corridor.

I begin to pray a simple prayer that God will be with me in the treatment room and that He will take away all fear. I climb up onto a tall, long bed where I lie with a large, cylindrical machine facing down at me. My new mask is placed over my face and then bolted and clamped to the bed, meaning that I can't move. The radiographers leave the room and talk to me via a speaker system from behind the thick lead wall. The radiation is fired in two sections. I can't really describe how it feels, but let's just say it is not pleasant. I don't have any immediate effects like the chemotherapy, but the effects of this will appear in the weeks to come.

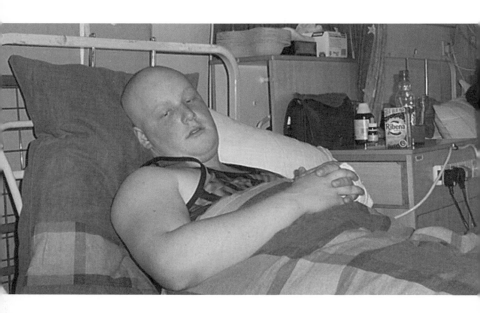

Chemotherapy and Radiotherapy take their effects,
draining the life from within me.

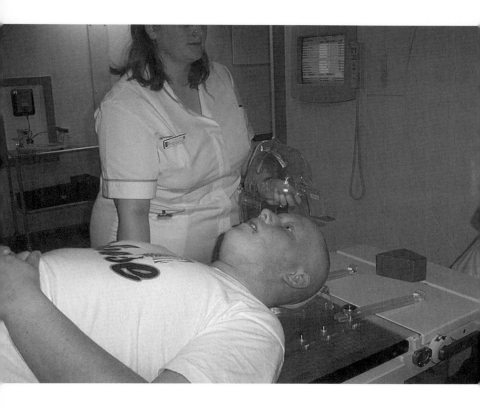

— LIFE OUT LOUD GUIDE —

 This chapter is the longest in the book and has still only scratched the surface of the events and emotions that were experienced. When writing this I was unsure If I really needed to go into all the details of the treatment and my experiences, but I made the decision that it was necessary – not to gain anyone's sympathy vote, but to highlight the severity of what we were facing.

Everyone has a story and every story needs to be told. Nothing of greatness has ever been achieved through mediocrity or by walking an easy path. In times of suffering we experience a God-given perseverance to overcome. This determination moulds and shapes our disposition, which leads to a wonderful word called "hope". Hope is the assurance that you will inherit the glory of God.

 THINK: OUT LOUD: What strikes you about what you have read?

How have you experienced God in your life? What story do you have to tell? How have you or others around experienced God through suffering? What kind of hope does this give you?

 READ: OUT LOUD: Romans 5:3-5 NIV
"Not only so, but we also glory in our sufferings, because we know that suffering produces perseverance; perseverance, character; and character, hope. And hope does not put us to shame, because God's love has been poured out into our hearts through the Holy Spirit, who has been given to us."

PRAY: OUT LOUD: Father, I thank you that even in times of suffering I know you are there and that you care. Help me to develop hope in my life. A true hope, based on who you are and what you are like. I ask that I would see all situations as opportunities to develop my character and to build hope, a lasting hope in the glory of God.

LIVE: OUT LOUD: This week share the story of what God has done and is doing in your life. If this is too hard at the moment then plan to share in the future.

CHAPTER 5
FACING THE FACTS

In striving to live our LIFE OUT LOUD we still have to face the facts. Unfortunately we are not exempt from them. They may sometimes shake us, but if addressed correctly they don't have the power to move us.

In defining the word "fact" there are two other words that are very helpful: evidence and significance. Each suggests that a fact is regarded as important when entering a situation or trying to reach a conclusion. In a court of law the facts are usually presented to the jury and it is based upon these that they make their decision. We cannot usually argue with the facts. They are very real and therefore need to be somewhat respected. A fact, however, in itself is certainly unable to tell the whole story.

Our life is constantly bombarded with "the facts". Facts are not necessarily a bad thing. It's our approach to the facts that determines their viability and affect on us. When relating this to my personal journey, I found that people in authority make statements and their words carry incredible weight. This is especially true in the field of medicine. Doctors and Consultants are rightly recognised as having expert knowledge in their particular field. Before I started the treatment my consultant presented me with a very long list of facts. Here were a few of them:

May lose my right eye

May have permanent loss of eyebrow

May have permanent loss of eyelashes

May lose sight in the right eye

May need a cataract operation

May have deformity to the face

May never have children naturally

May have skin burns

May have damage to the pituitary gland

May have damage to the surface of my eye

May have damage to the tear ducts

May have further kidney problems

May have mouth ulcers

May need blood transfusions

May lose my life...

A list of facts like this is enough to give anyone a few sleepless nights. So when we are presented with the facts what do we do? First, we listen politely to the consultant whose duty it is to inform me of all the eventualities. Smile, maybe even nod your head acknowledging that you understand the facts. But all the time remember that they may know a lot, but they don't know it all. They know numbers and statistics, but they don't know you. Only one person knows you well enough. He even knows the number of hairs on your head, your deepest thoughts and your secret dreams. Thankfully, Jesus has the final word not your consultant. Shake the consultant's hand and thank God for them.

Apart from medical conditions, facts can be foremost in other times of trial. It may be your bank manager informing you about some financial situation, like a debt you cannot resolve. It may be your employer delivering the news of an unexpected redundancy. It could even be facts surrounding a broken marriage that suggest it's beyond repair. The next step is look at the list of facts set out before you and, if you remember nothing else from this chapter, please remember this: we never deny the facts. I will say that one more time. We never deny the facts. Those reading this who have a faith in God may already be rising up on the inside, thinking that this comment shows a lack of faith.

Allow me to explain. A phrase that comes to mind is burying our head in the sand – the simple naivety of thinking that if we can't see the problem, then the problem can't see us. In fact, we can operate in faith whilst acknowledging the facts. Refusing to acknowledge the facts is a refusal to acknowledge and confront the situation. And if we don't do that, then how are we supposed to ask God to intervene? As previously mentioned, I asked Mum if I could just run away from my problem and believe God for an instantaneous miracle. We all really wanted to, but if we had done it would have been highly irresponsible.

Here are some other guidelines for facing facts when dealing with an illness:

Avoiding medical advice

We will inevitably get a range of different opinions from different medical minds on certain issues, but as confusing as that can be, we certainly shouldn't avoid medical guidance. God has ordained the medical profession for a reason. The local church, God's house and God's people, has historically been the longest running provider of healthcare, way before there were hospitals or nursing homes. We put our trust in God, be we also have to place a level of trust in people who have been put there to help us.

Refusing Medication

My personal view is that we should not refuse the appropriate medical treatment required on the grounds of it signifying a lack of faith. If you have heard the audible voice of God telling you to decline treatment and you tell me you are just believing for the healing – that is something I could never argue with. However, in reality I would imagine that is not always the case.

God created this earth and from it have emerged many naturally occurring medicines. Healing is usually a process and also a combination of God's grace and favour, along with the outstanding wonders of medicine. Why not use what He has created? I will touch on this more later in the book. Whether we are dealing with illness or some other challenge, we can apply these same broad principles when getting to grips with the facts.

Avoiding medical advice may translate into avoiding professional council. It may be your financial advisor, church pastor or marriage counsellor proposing a plan within their remit of expertise that you choose to side step, because you think you can do it on your own or you simply don't want to face the facts. This is similar to refusing medication. The good news is that the Bible says that wisdom comes in the abundance of council. This means that you don't always have to rely on one person to tell you the answer.

This chapter may have seemed a little heavy, but it is an important issue to discuss. If I were to end the book here, then hope would soon desert us. We will never win battles in life just by facing the facts. We have to face the facts, but we certainly don't have to embrace them. The facts don't define us; God defines us. There is something, someone for us to embrace, that is bigger and higher than the facts – a force that outweighs facts every single time. Facts occupy the natural realm. But through a personal relationship with Jesus Christ we have access to another realm – a supernatural realm – which is the truth.

Facts = Natural

Truth = Supernatural

We face the facts, but because of Jesus we can embrace the truth.

At the end of my treatment, still facing the facts

—LIFE OUT LOUD GUIDE—

In summary, in my situation some facts appeared a little more daunting than others and the outcomes still remained unanswered. The "fact" that, if I lived, my life might have some limitations on it got me thinking. Physically, would I look completely different? Would I have a right eye? Would I ever find a wife who could love me and accept me with all the "labels" that might come to define me? Would I ever be able to hold my own child and know the joy of being called Dad? But this one thing I believed for sure: when God enters a situation He does not leave it half finished.

THINK: OUT LOUD: What strikes you about what you have read?

What do you think is the difference between facing the facts and embracing them? How did the revelation of facts being natural and TRUTH being SUPERNATURAL change your perspective? How do you think you embrace the truth in your life and situations?

READ: OUT LOUD: John 3:16 NIV:

"For God so loved the world that he gave his one and only Son, that whoever believes in him shall not perish but have eternal life. For God did not send his Son into the world to condemn the world, but to save the world through him."

PRAY: OUT LOUD: Father, I thank you that you love us and actively care for us. I pray and ask that I would be able to embrace your truth fully, not to hide from the facts but to see that your truth is bigger and greater. Thank you for the truth of Jesus and that in Him all things are restored and made whole. May I embrace this truth today.

 LIVE: OUT LOUD: Think about situations you are facing at the moment. Speak positively about them (see chapter 2) and speak words of truth from Jesus: I am loved, I am a child of God, I am whole. Allow these words to help you embrace the truth.

CHAPTER 6
EMBRACING TRUTH

To live LIFE OUT LOUD this chapter is a winner for you. If you get it and believe it the famous saying really does become true: "anything is possible".

Once we get the revelation that the truth always outweighs the facts our approach to situations quickly changes. A new lease of life enters our spirit, urging us to carry on the fight because there is always something that can supersede our natural circumstances. Let's have a quick look back at the list of facts that I was presented with when starting my treatment. If this principle is real, and not just a good thought, then the information below provides strong proof that in God's economy facts must submit to truth:

May lose my right eye: I am looking at my computer screen writing this chapter with not one but two eyes. Repeat this line after me ... The truth is higher than the facts!

May have permanent loss of eyebrow and eyelashes: When God designed and created my body He used eyebrows and eyelashes. My body has come back in alignment with God's creativity, meaning that my eyebrows and eyelashes have fully returned. The truth is higher then the facts!

May lose sight in the right eye: My right eye has a little blurring in the vision, but I can still see. The truth is higher then the facts!

May have deformity to the face: No deformity to the right hand side of my face. Come on, say it again ... The truth is higher then the facts!

May have permanent skin burns: Due to the intense radio therapy my skin could have been permanently damaged, but if Shadrach, Meshach and Abednego could walk through a fiery furnace and not be burnt I could have radiation and not be burnt. So this is what we prayed for and this is what happened. You know what's coming now ... The truth is higher then the facts!

May have damage to the pituitary gland: This may have caused problems in relation to physical growth, but the truth is, I am 5ft 10" and weigh around 200lb of pure steel. All together now ... The truth is higher then the facts!

May have damage to the surface of my eye and tear ducts: My eye requires drops every 3-4 hours every day and I may have to continue this for the rest of my life. But this is such a small price to pay. After a recent visit to the hospital my consultant saw signs of the surface of my eye actually starting to heal. Healing is a process!

And by the way, my tear ducts are fine; I can cry like anyone else. Shout it out ... The truth is higher then the facts!

May have further kidney problems: No problems ever experienced with my kidneys. Scream it out ... The truth is higher then the facts!

May have serious mouth ulcers during treatment: Never had one mouth ulcer during treatment. And again ... The truth is higher then the facts!

May need multiple blood transfusions: Never had a single blood transfusion. One last time and this time say it like you mean it ... The truth is higher then the facts!

Here is a challenge for you. Wherever you are reading this book now I want you to shout out, "The truth is higher then the facts." Even if you are in the middle of Starbucks enjoying your coffee, even if you are in the quiet carriage of the train, even if the kids are asleep upstairs in bed ... just try it. It will make you feel better, but it will also be very funny.

This is the point in the chapter where your faith levels have risen so high that you just can't stop shouting and clapping! You may well be out of your seat, standing and waving a small white handkerchief shouting, "Preach it Pastor Dave!" Well, maybe our American readers at least. The British readers amongst us will be a little more reserved. Perhaps a small ripple of applause is in order, but the handkerchief remains firmly in the pocket.

Now we have all calmed down we need to get back to business. The more astute readers may have noticed that a few facts were missing from the list compared to that given in the previous chapter. I needed to address these issues separately to help bring clarity and context.

When you look at the list above you will see that every fact has had to bow its knee to the truth, which is just incredible. However, being a Christian on planet earth is like living in a gap between two worlds. The Bible tells us to pray for the Kingdom to come on earth, suggesting that the Kingdom of heaven is not yet here in all its fullness. Every time a fact presents itself in the natural and the truth prevails the Kingdom of heaven touches earth. When Jesus walked this very earth, once again the power of the Kingdom came in fullness. However ... living in the gap can frustrate us when we don't see the breakthrough manifest. This means that we need to pray for the Kingdom to collide with earth more and more in the days ahead.

Back to the remaining facts. I was told that my right eye might have a cataract form due to the radiotherapy. I wanted to be able to tick this one off my list too, but sadly I did have to have cataract surgery. I have no doubt that God could have sorted it for me, but I needed to go through another process to receive healing. I had the operation and now have a plastic lens. You know what, it was one of the easiest things to go through compared to all the rest. I actually quite enjoyed it! The final remaining facts were closely linked. The prospects of getting married and, finally, the ability to have children.

I finish this chapter with those two statements, which were unanswered at this stage of my journey. God's plans are always to prosper us and never to harm us, so I knew that He wanted the very best for me. For now I had to rest in this and trust that He was in control.

Comparing this photo to the previous one really does highlight that there actually is a God! Overwhelming gratitude for what Jesus has done for me.

—LIFE OUT LOUD GUIDE—

In summary, the facts said that Dave Bell had been diagnosed with a life-threatening illness that may well cut his life short at the age of 16. The truth was that Jesus Christ hung on a cross 2,000 years ago so that Dave Bell could live his life in complete freedom. The truth always outweighs the facts.

THINK: OUT LOUD: What strikes you about what you have read? SHOUT IT OUT!

How did you feel reading the statements and shouting "The truth outweighs the facts"? Are there situations and circumstances that you need to declare God's truth over? Who have you got standing with you in this?

READ: OUT LOUD: Romans 8:38-39:
"For I am sure that neither death nor life, nor angels nor rulers, nor things present nor things to come, nor powers, nor height nor depth, nor anything else in all creation, will be able to separate us from the love of God in Christ Jesus our Lord."

PRAY: OUT LOUD: Father, I thank you for the truth that we cannot be separated from your love for us. I know that you love me and that through Christ Jesus I am called your child. Help me to stand in the truth of your love and embrace it above all the facts or circumstances in my life.

LIVE: OUT LOUD: The Christian life is not one that we do on our own. Make sure you have others around you who will support and love you through any situation you face.

CHAPTER 7
PRAYER OUT LOUD
- STUART BELL

One of the biggest changes in our thinking took place in the arena of prayer. We needed to move from "saying our prayers" to faith-filled praying. This involved the regular declaring of promises that we received from the Bible.

I still have pages of promises that were written down during that period which remind me of God's faithfulness. God gifted us in Lincoln with wonderful people who stood with us, strongly and boldly. I thank God particularly for God's gift to us of Nigerian believers who helped us learn a new way of praying. This often took us out of our comfort zones and into a faith zone where we simply knew our prayers were being answered. This was not to do with a new formula, but with moving us into a new level of confidence.

In fact, I'd be bold enough to say that I believe God gave us a strategy as to how to pray. We outlined some of this in the book

Mud in the Eye, but suffice to say our goals in prayer were both clear and measurable. God spoke so clearly into this strategy that we knew we weren't just clutching at straws or making things up. For those who are interested, I still pray the same prayer every morning asking for protection over every area of Dave's body. I don't see this as a religious observance, but a confession of faith and trust in God.

I am still amazed at how God guided us through the story of the man who was born blind. This story released us from the nagging possibility that this terrible sickness had come upon us due to some sin in the family. The combination of mud and divine spit helped us grapple with the difficult decisions to do with chemo and radiotherapy. We ultimately give God our thanks for healing, but recognise the wonderful work of people within the NHS.

During those months I learned not only the power of thought-through prayer and strategies, but also of the gifts of the Holy Spirit, particularly speaking in tongues. I began to learn that "speaking in tongues" really does edify or build up a person and I was conscious on occasions that battles were being won in an invisible world when we prayed in the spirit. The following story illustrates how this practically worked out during a particularly hard day.

When Dave woke one Monday morning, as light touched his eye, almost unbearable pain caused him to cry out. The tissue of the surface of his eye was bright red and clearly he was in considerable discomfort. Though Dave resisted the thought of going back to hospital it wasn't long before he was happy that we contacted the ophthalmic ward at Leicester Royal Infirmary. They asked us to get to Leicester as soon as possible.

We were soon in the car and ready for off. As I pressed the accelerator, Dave, in a slightly provocative manner said, "Well aren't you going to pray then?" I instantly thought up a fairly standard prayer followed by a sentence or two of tongues. "Is that is then?" he then asked. Being corrected by your son requires grace, so I quietly asked what he had in mind. "I expected you would put a bit more energy into it!" he replied, then added, "Speaking in tongues really helps."

So I began speaking in tongues out loud to convince Dave that I was really praying. He sat back with eyes closed in order that the sunlight didn't bring him pain. For a while, if I'm honest, I spoke in tongues in the car in response to Dave's request, but after a while I noticed things began to change.

I realise that, at this point, my story becomes pretty subjective and I'm also aware I may lose some readers at this point. However, perhaps I could put it like this: our journey would take us through Newark and then on a dual carriageway to Leicester. I began with "Lincoln faith", and by this I mean I was praying simply because I should. There was no real sense of anointing or faith. However, after about half an hour I moved into "Newark faith". Praying had become easier. I was aware of God's presence and that He was with us in our struggles. I was also aware that He was carrying some of our pain. After around an hour and a half with only a few traffic frustrations we moved into "Leicester faith" and as we instantly found a parking space (a minor miracle in itself) our levels of expectation were high.

David's pain had receded and after a short and amicable

consultation we returned to Lincoln with some steroid drops to help the conjunctivitis that had been caused through radiotherapy. David never had a day of pain like it again and we learned that there is such a thing as wrestling in prayer until we get a breakthrough (Colossians 4:12). During that journey the decibel levels of my intercessions did raise considerably, but I'm convinced that added volume was more for my benefit than the Lord's, since the Scriptures make it clear that He is not hard of hearing.

Since that day prayer times have on occasions carried a different dimension. I do believe that there is something very powerful when a whole church prays out loud together. As Christians we are sometimes described as "loud mouthed", but in the West we do need to discover the "loud voiced" Church.

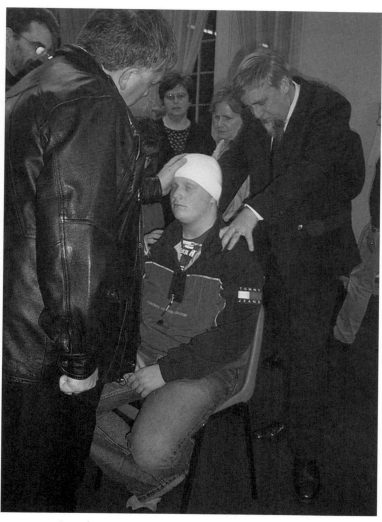

One of our many prayer meetings. Prayer works. Try it.

—LIFE OUT LOUD GUIDE—

THINK: OUT LOUD: What strikes you about what you have read?

How do you view prayer? What issues most cause you to pray? Have you used praying out loud or in tongues before? How might you seek to use these more?

READ: OUT LOUD: Psalm 17:6-7:

"I call on you, my God, for you will answer me; turn your ear to me and hear my prayer. Show me the wonders of your great love, you who save by your right hand those who take refuge in you from their foes.."

PRAY: OUT LOUD: Father, I thank you that you carry my pain and suffering and that you are with me. Help me to learn to pray and at times to battle for breakthrough in areas where it is needed. I open myself up to you for you to teach me. I ask for people to stand alongside me. May the God of breakthrough be active in my life.

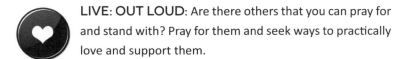

LIVE: OUT LOUD: Are there others that you can pray for and stand with? Pray for them and seek ways to practically love and support them.

CHAPTER 8
WEDDING BELLS

When you stare into a hospital mirror to see a reflection of bald, pale, overweight cancer patient staring back at you, the idea of someone ever loving you is a dream. I never thought it would become a reality. I could never imagine looking again how I use to look or even my eye returning to how it was. I had to prepare for the fact that I may not have a right eyebrow or eyelash or could even have some deformity to the bone structure in my face.

The idea of having a girlfriend was a distant one. It was somewhere in the back of my mind, but considering the circumstances I never really entertained the idea. I just assumed that no one would be attracted to me.

When out with friends I would mostly sit quietly in a corner, wearing my hat, hoping that no one would notice that I had rather a lack of hair for the average 16 year old and some problem with my eye.

In the summer of 2004 Duane and Kris White hosted "Launch" – a youth missions program. The week of training was held in Lincoln and then all the delegates were sent out across the world. I hadn't planned on going, but after a few chats with my godfather I decided to book in at the last minute. One possible motive was that I knew there could be a few girls going and I think that swayed me.

For one reason or another I was late for the event registration so I went straight into the evening meal. I walked into the room and had a quick look around to see lots of new faces, but then, time stood still. Sat over in the corner was what can only be described as "one hot unit". (Note to any international readers: this terminology can only be translated as "one hot unit"!) I immediately assumed that she must be American or live miles away from me. Nevertheless, I plucked up the courage to go over and speak to her later that night.

I asked her name and where she was from, expecting to hear an American accent. "Sarah," she quietly replied with an English accent, "...from Grimsby," she added. Hold the phone ... Grimsby ... that's only 40 minutes away from Lincoln. I did then begin to think to myself, surely something this pretty cannot have come from Grimsby. It was too good to be true! I later realised that we had also both been to Grapevine for the last 16 years and never seen each other. She had also been to an Atlas concert, but I never saw her there either. Sarah was going on the trip to Kenya. I wasn't, so I asked if I could come and see her when she got back. Her reply wasn't exactly what I was after, but in a round about way she eventually said that I could.

The day arrived and I managed to convince Dad that it would help my cause if I picked her up in his Audi. We spent the day together and eventually it was time for me to leave. I tried to linger before getting back into the car to see if I was going to get a little kiss, but she wasn't having any of it! I told her that I liked her and to my surprise she said she liked me too. I thought the whole "...as a friend" speech was going to follow, but it didn't. I was in there!

The next time we met was at the Grapevine set up week, where I offered my services in the white-lining department, marking out spaces for all the tents. This was only because Sarah was doing it. I wasn't really interested in white-lining in all honesty. This is when the first embarrassing story comes in.

Sarah and I were walking towards the exhibition centre one afternoon, only to find a massive pool of water blocking the entrance. Any normal person would possibly have used a different entrance or tried in some way to avoid the large quantity of muddy water. But no, not me. I had to try and act cool in front of Sarah, so I attempted to leap over the water.

I went for it, but gravity took its effect quicker than I had estimated. I not only landed in the centre of what can only be described as a full on pond, but I had to reach across and grab Sarah to stop myself from fully submerging as I lost all sense of balance. Sarah's overall physique is slightly different to mine in that she weighs about half what I do, so you can picture her attempting to hold me up.

I don't easily get embarrassed, but this occasion made my cheeks a little bit red. On the final night of Grapevine, however, Sarah and I officially started dating ... praise the Lord!

The Engagement

Two years later I decided that it was time for me to think about asking the question. I can remember talking to Mum and Dad and saying that I was going to ask Sarah's Dad if I could marry his daughter. I was slightly nervous that Dave (Sarah's dad) was going to ask me some in depth spiritual and biblical questions on marriage, so I got the Dad to give me some good answers to overcome any possible problems. I was all set!

The night I decided to ask Dave was nerve wracking. Put it this way, I've never been so nervous in all my life! I walked in and out of his office about six times before I even said a word! Eventually, I stopped being a girl and asked him the question. He asked me in a stern voice, "Give me three good reasons why you should marry my daughter!"

It wasn't the response I had planned in my head. I was thinking that a simple "Yes" would suffice or something along those lines. I started to stutter something about believing that God had brought us together and that we could accomplish more together than we could apart. Then I thought I would further warm him up by appealing to his Christian viewpoint and started quoting the Bible passage that says it is better to marry than burn with passion! Thanks for that one, Dad, it worked a treat! Before I could come up with a third reason, Dave put me out of my misery and stopped me. He said yes, of course I could marry his daughter. He then prayed for me and gave me his blessing, which I thought was an amazing thing.

The next Grapevine was the time I had chosen to propose. It was the last day of the event and I had arranged for a team of people to help me decorate some of the gardens. I had a big archway full of fairy lights and candles everywhere. Leading from the archway was a little gazebo with champagne, chocolates and our favourite song playing. I put on my suit and waited for her under the archway. It had all gone to plan; she arrived without knowing a thing.

The Wedding

For most people of my age talking about marriage would be quite straightforward – you either want to get married or you don't. But I had to have a conversation with Sarah that most people would never have, especially someone my age. We had to talk about the facts again, the possibility of not being able to have children. I felt quite worthless and ashamed of actually having to say these words to her; to someone who had a big love of children. But when somebody tells you that it doesn't make them feel any different about you and they still love you just the same – that is an amazing thing. Together we believed that this prospect was only a fact. The truth was, God could turn this situation around for His glory and maybe we would still be able to have children.

The wedding plans where underway and this distant dream was nearly in reach. The big day arrived. Against all the odds I was going to get married. I had four best friends as best men: my Dad, my brother Andrew, my brother-in-law Glen and my cousin Ben. In addition to this I had 10 of my closest friends as ushers (slightly excessive but who cares!). Sarah had five bridesmaids and two little flower girls.

All the best men and ushers lined up at the back of the church. I looked out onto a massive crowd of people. It was unbelievable. The music came on and we all walked down in a row to the Top Gun theme tune. Can you guess whose idea that was? I wrote the piece of music that Sarah was to walk down the aisle to. Me being me, I did it the night before, not the best idea in the world. The music started to play and one by one the bridesmaids walked down. Finally, the moment arrived when I saw Sarah. Words can't describe how beautiful she looked. My eyes started to fill up. More than anything it was the fact that this was real life, not a dream.

Dad had a few roles that day. Not only was he my best man, but he also married us. The ceremony began and I was doing well until he spoke the line, "In sickness and in health." I had to pause and fight back the tears. This line was a struggle.

The reception was held at the Lincolnshire Show Ground. This was an amazing venue for us as this was the place where we first started going out and also the place where we got engaged. This was one of the best days of my life; I didn't want it to end.

Since I missed some of my teenage years due to illness I have decided that it is completely acceptable to live those lost years for the duration of my life. In other words, I will be 16 every day. This is a wonderful prospect for me, but it does have an effect on my wife, Sarah. One good example is the time when we were invited round to my parent's house for dinner with a few other guests. Sarah was sat in a full living room, chatting with my parent's friends in a very friendly and dignified manner. I, on the other hand, had conveniently excused myself from the boring discussions to go and sit in the tree house that I built.

I told everyone that I built this tree house for my nephew, Jermac, but it was actually built by me for me. I sat there for a good few hours shooting unsuspecting birds with my BB gun. For the record, I only injured one pigeon which later flew away as if nothing had happened. So, all in all, Bear Grylls would not have been happy.

Another aspect of this is that I rarely back out of a challenge. This was proven on our last family holiday to the coast. Picture the scene: All of the family having a wonderful bonding experience on a beautiful summer's day on the glorious British coast line. Sorry, the spirit of an evangelist has already come over me and I have already extended the truth of my illustration. Controversial. A beautiful summer's day here in the UK is just above freezing and a British beech resort is usually a suitable habitat for a farmyard animal. Anyway... a certain family member, no names mentioned, but she is my only sister, challenged me to take all of my clothes off – except the Calvin's – and run along the beech, which was at the time filled with young families and grandparents.

The culmination of the challenge was to dive into the deserted North Sea. The reason why no one was swimming at the time is because they were obviously a little smarter then me. I embraced this challenge with open arms and, like a leaping gazelle, ran across the beech wearing nothing but my underpants and a smile. My nephews thought that this was the greatest thing they'd ever witnessed. Sarah, however, looked on with discomfort and embarrassment. In summary, a word of advice to anyone thinking about doing this: don't wear white underpants.

Sarah, you have made my life complete and I thank God for you every day. I could never imagine someone loving me like you do, with all the "labels" over my life, but you have looked past all of these. Thank you for loving me just how I am. You are my best friend and I love every second I have with you.

I love you.

Yes, I know what you're thinking ... I married way out of my league! The beautiful Sarah. The ladies standing either side of Sarah and I are some of the nurses from Ward 27 who cared for me during my treatment. What an incredible image.

CHAPTER 9
MIRACLES

I've always wanted to be a Dad. I love the idea. Love the thought of having a little companion who I could teach to be the next soccer superstar or the lead guitarist of the next big rock band. Okay, yes, I did want a little boy first. There is nothing wrong with girls, of course, but I suppose thinking as the future father I wanted to be, a boy would have been just perfect to start the family. I think having such a good relationship with my dad made me very aware of what a joy the father and son bond can be. I wanted a child to experience what I have experienced from a loving Dad. But constantly, in the back of my mind, my thoughts would tell me that this might not be possible.

As I mentioned, when I asked Sarah to marry me we couldn't just have the usual conversation that most engaged couples do. We couldn't dive straight into a discussion about bridesmaids, choice of colours or best men. First we had to discuss something more serious. Once again I had to get out the long list of facts which, as we've already learnt, we have to face. The words that had to come out of my mouth were not easy to say: "Sarah, if you choose to marry me, you have to understand that we may not be able to have children naturally."

I felt quite worthless having to say this and she did not deserve to have to hear it. "I'm only 20 years old," I thought, "so why do I have to say this?" Just to add another perspective to this already difficult situation, the hand I was asking in marriage was the hand of a midwife. Sarah was delivering new born babies every day of the week as a profession. Aside from that, we are also talking about a woman who has a fond love of children.

Her response to my statement immediately highlighted one thing to me: she had faith. Without any hesitation or further questions she made it very clear that this did not change anything. We would stand together believing that God would come through for us one last time. What an incredible woman.

During the prayer sessions I had during my treatment, the issue of fertility was addressed quite strongly. It's an embarrassing subject when you are standing in the middle of a circle of intercessors. One of our Nigerian pray-ers suggested one night that we should pray for my "loins". I wasn't too sure what my "loins" were at first. I said that this was fine as long as we prohibited the "laying on of hands", especially by the male contingent.

After a few giggles, however, the group began to pray into my future, believing that I would be able to have children. One of the intercessors came forward to give a prophetic word. The interesting thing about this particular prayer was that she was the midwife who actually delivered me! She was the very first person to see me enter the world. Interesting. She then explained her vision. She saw me sat at a kitchen table in a house wearing a suit and reading the paper – not alone, but with children. One sat on my knee and the others sat at the table.

At first I thought this could not be correct, as I could never imagine myself reading a newspaper – now that really would be a miracle! In which case, maybe this really was a God-given image meant to infuse another level of faith to believe that He would come through.

Now let's skip forward in the story, which brings us into the first few years of marriage. I can remember travelling as a young musician and playing guitar for various worship artists. On one of my travels I had a prophetic word from a gentleman in the congregation. The meeting itself was a little wild and full of weird and wonderful people – more weird than wonderful in all honesty. At the end of the meeting, as I was packing away my guitar a man approached me. Without any form of introduction, and in a raised voice, he looked me in the eye and shouted in my face, "FERTILITY!"

At first I laughed since this was such a bizarre and unusual greeting – and he also said it in a thick Yorkshire accent. "THE WORD IS FERTILITY" he repeated. I thought for a second that this must be a patient on the loose from the local mental hospital ... then It hit me. As "interesting" as this man was, I actually think it may have been from God. He later went on to say that I would be able to have children and not to worry. He said this not knowing anything about me or my situation. As soon as I got home I told Sarah and our faith levels rose a little higher.

Now married for two years we started to think about our future together. Like most newlyweds we had our five-year plan mapped out, full of adventures and experiences ideally suited for a young married couple. We spoke about children as something in the distance.

I won't lie by saying all worry was eradicated and an inner certainty rose up every time the subject of children was mentioned. That didn't happen. However, I did have an inner peace about the situation; the peace of knowing that it was out of my hands and all we could do was to pray. This one fact was still on the list that remained unanswered. But unless we present God with the impossible, we will never see a miracle.

During my treatment I wore the same t-shirt in hospital. It was given to me at a church conference and there was nothing too special about it other than it had my name written on the back. This t-shirt was with me in some of my darkest hours and for that very reason I decided to keep it in a drawer as another valuable piece of the journey. However, it came out of the draw one day, but this time for a very different reason...

The 24th of August 2009 was a special day for Sarah and I. A historic day. A day that will be remembered for all the days to come. A day of answered prayer. A day of great joy and fulfilment. A day where the facts once again became subject to the truth.

It was the day that Sarah gave birth to our miracle baby, Jackson. The phrase "God is good" is a big understatement. Words worthy of describing what He has done for us have not yet been invented. Little Jackson entered the world weighing 8lbs. One translation of the name Jackson means "God has been gracious and shown favour". The other translation is "the son of Jack". I chose to ignore that one for obvious reasons. In case you were wondering where the t-shirt went, Sarah was wearing it whilst giving birth to our miracle son.

Becoming a father has changed me in many ways. I still have the mind of a 16 year old, so don't worry, but it has shown me the love that God has for me in a very different light. God loves me just as I love Jackson. His feelings for me are the feelings I have towards Jackson. Yet God's love for me is greater; so great that He allowed His only son to die so that I could live. So that in turn I could have my own child.

I'll end this chapter with a great story. A true one. I still go to the hospital for check ups and on a recent visit I thought it would be appropriate to take Jackson with me. We got in the car and did the familiar journey from Lincoln to Leicester. We arrived and, with the J-dog (Jackson), by my side we got into the elevator. I picked him up and he pressed that customary button for the 4th floor.

The doors opened and we walked towards the big wooden doors that were hiding the world of Ward 27. We opened the doors and walked onto the ward, hand in hand, with my beautiful wife close behind and also accompanied by Jackson's Mama and Dada (my parents). I picked Jackson up and we knocked on the consultant's door. When he opened the door he was quite taken back. To see me in the condition I am in is quite unheard of, but for me to be holding a perfectly healthy baby boy in my right arm was something that he had not yet seen in his entire career.

The facts say that Jackson should not be here today. So as a new family we are very thankful for the truth. Jackson is incredible and you will all be pleased to know that he has his mother's looks, but like me, relishes any opportunity to take all his clothes off.

I end this chapter with one last piece of recent news. On Sunday June 2, 2013, the t-shirt came out of the drawer again and Sarah gave birth to our second miracle baby – Levi Lincoln Bell. COME ON!!!

Jackson and his Daddy.
My Miracle boy.
Thankfully, he has his
mother's good looks.

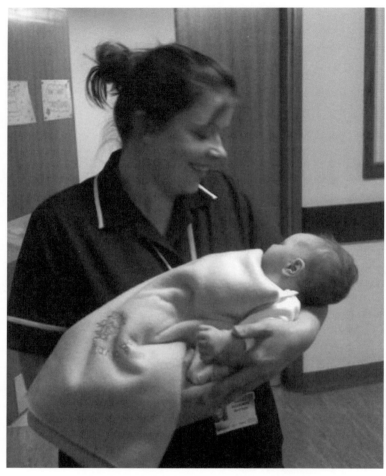

The sister of Ward 27 holding my miracle son.
If you're not crying at this one there is something clinically wrong with you.

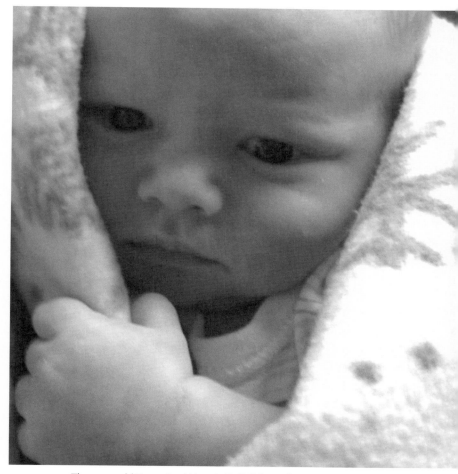

The new addition – Levi Lincoln Bell. What a beauty.

CHAPTER 10
HEALING IS ON ITS WAY

When we choose to live LIFE OUT LOUD we have to realise that we may not know all the answers to life's big questions. This is fine. We don't need to know all the answers. If we knew them all that would make us God ... and the good news is, we're not.

Here is another disclaimer for you. My theology is pretty simple. So for me to give you some grand theological insight into the mystery that is healing would be a little unwise. Sometimes though, when I hear someone ask the question: "Why was my prayer for healing not answered?" and hear the many different responses from different people, I want to put forward my own theological explanation. I think I may have come up with the best answer of them all, and it is only three words long. Ready for it?

I don't know.

The simplicity of this statement is what makes the answer so profound, whether you realise it or not. It's not a personal excuse for not tackling the big question – it's just an honest answer. If we all knew the right answer to this people wouldn't still be asking the same question! It is still one of the most asked questions by non-believers or by those who are searching for faith.

Although ultimately "I don't know", at one level I do know some things. Having received healing myself I can try to explain my personal experiences. The big mystery of physical healing is only really to do with one thing: timing. It is not a debate about whether miracles actually happen today, because they do. The incredible news is that Jesus Christ is still in the business of healing 2,000 years on. This is not just a phenomenon that was only available for the characters we read about in the Bible. It is available for all of us in this day and age. We just need to learn how that healing is manifest in our lifetime. The good news is, one way or another you will still receive your healing. I like to approach it by talking about the 4 P's.

Perspective

The first "P" is perspective. We need to get our perspective and thinking right from the outset. Upon receiving my diagnosis I had two clear choices to make. I either got angry with God and chose to fight this thing by myself or I acknowledged that I served a healing God whose plans are to always prosper and not to harm me; a God who could walk me through.

It is an easy and obvious decision on paper, but on hearing life-changing news, we have the tendency to get wrapped up in the emotion of the events and forget the many years of God's faithfulness to us. So often we take one challenging event out of context, compared to the bigger picture of God's continued goodness to us.

Once we have established that we need God's help, we then have to understand the reasons why this may be happening or, perhaps, why God is allowing this to happen. Many people will pose certain questions at this stage, such as: "Is this due to some past sin? ... Is it because of something in my family line? ... Is God picking on me/testing me?" and so the list continues.

When I was on the ward ready for my eye biopsy I opened the bedside cupboard to find a Bible. I opened it with a simple prayer that God would speak to me. Like most of us would admit to doing at times, we can open the Bible at random, hoping it will land on a page that is relevant for us at that moment. Usually, however, it lands on some random bit of Leviticus or an unusual proverb such as "As a dog returns to its vomit, so a fool repeats his folly" (Proverbs 31:6). What? Anyway, not helpful!

On this occasion though, I flipped the Bible open at the story of the man who was born blind. This one passage of Scripture answered all of my questions. The disciples even asked the frequently asked questions for us. "Rabbi, who sinned, this man or his parents, that he was born blind." This question deals swiftly with the issues of past sin, sin in the family line and personal conviction. Jesus then replies, "Neither this man nor his parents sinned that he was born blind, but this happened so that the work of God may be displayed in his life." Wow. This meant that my problem was never God's intention and was definitely not His doing. However, God was going to allow me to walk through it so that His work could be displayed in the process. The Bible also says that God will never take you down a path that your character can't handle, so whatever the process is and whatever the path you have to walk ... you can do it.

With physical healing I see three types: Power, Process and Partnership.

Power

I still believe in what I would call the "overnight miracle", where God heals within the blink of an eye, but mostly in the western world we don't tend to see as much of this as we should. I don't fully know why this is, but if I had to hazard a guess it may simply come down to our levels of faith. My reason for thinking this is that often when a healing takes place in the Bible Jesus says, "Your faith has healed you" or "Your faith has set you free." He doesn't say, "Your geographical location has healed you"! But living here in the UK means that we don't always have to rely on God to provide for our every need. We usually have access to food and water. We have the Health Service with enough medication and skilled individuals who offer great advice. So If we become sick with a common virus we have everything in place to make a recovery. However, people living in a part of the world where these basic amenities do not exist only have one hope and that's Jesus.

The Bible is full of miracles that were instant. From the parting of the Red Sea and the feeding of the five thousand through to raising Lazarus from the dead and even a talking donkey! My viewpoint is to always start by believing and praying for this first. Even through the telling of my story and through some of the worship songs I have written we have seen these types of miracles first hand.

A lady in our church, who was very new to the faith, received a serious diagnosis of cancer. After praying for her we were later informed that the results of the next scan showed that the tumour had completely disappeared. This was nothing less than a miracle.

One of my favourite stories is to do with a close friend of mine. I met him when he had stage 4 cancer and the doctors had given no signs of any hope. He is a world-class pianist and, as I watched him play his piano whilst pushing through the pain and discomfort caused by such a terrible disease, it started to trouble me. I knew I had to pray for him. He had decided to sell his classic car, as he did not want his wife to have any financial burdens when he was gone. This troubled me even more! I prayed for him personally at every possible opportunity. Our only hope was Jesus. I can report to you today that my good friend does not need to sell that classic car any more as he is completely whole. Thank you Jesus.

Process

I have become very aware that healing, in most cases, will be a process. Where there is process there is usually unrest and frustration. We can be very impatient people who want to see the results now, and the idea of having to go through a process can make us lose sight of reaching the end result. In reality, the process is the important part – just as important as receiving the healing.

Even though I prayed every night for my situation to be sorted by the morning, God decided that the process would be more beneficial to me in the long run. My theory is that you will never forget a time of trial, but you may forget a quickly answered prayer. There is a good example of this in the Bible where we read about the ten lepers who were instantly healed. This was great, but of the ten men, only one remembered to thank Jesus. Maybe this ratio would have been different if they'd had to walk a longer path? We also read the story of Naaman, who was also a leper. In order to receive his healing he had to walk many miles and then dip his body seven times in the muddy waters of the river Jordan. Not once, but seven times. What is interesting here is that Naaman would have preferred any other river to go to than the muddy waters of the river Jordan. Clearly God was dealing with something in him.

Constant prayer at every possible opportunity is key. Get yourself into every prayer line, sign up to the church prayer list, attend the prayer meetings, even if you don't feel like it. When we go to the doctors for some antibiotics we are always told to take the whole course. It's the same with prayer: keep taking it until you see the change.

Partnership

I am also very aware that prayer is a partnership. My healing came through a combination of God's grace and provision working hand in hand with the outstanding medical profession. Most of the chemotherapy I received came from natural ingredients that we see around us here on planet earth. God created the earth and in it made provisions with me and you in mind that could aid the healing process. God not only created these resources, He then ordained the scientists/medical practitioners who researched, discovered them and then administered them. The

God-given calling on their lives played a part in my healing and they don't even realise it.

Below is a very simple healing check list which may position you a little better to start to see results. This is not the whole answer, but it is certainly part of it.

Healing Check-list

- Get prayer on every possible occasion
- Surround yourself with faith-filled people
- Confess your sins
- Choose forgiveness and build any broken relationships
- Read the Scriptures daily
- Listen to worship music
- Speak positively
- Keep your faith levels high
- Get the leaders of the church to anoint you with oil

To end this chapter I have included the lyrics to another song written by Chris Eaton, Abby Eaton and myself, called "Healing is on its way". God has sent your healing ... It's on its way.

Just another everyday as sun comes up
Tragedy and ecstasy lie in wait for us
Are you walking through the fire, crying out no more?
Is your world turned upside down, overwhelmed by the storm?

Don't give up
Don't give up

Healing, is on its way
Our God is the God who saves
My Healing, is on its way
Jesus Christ name above all names

Who can know or understand why it has to be
Take your pain by the hand and set it free
If I had my chance again I would not change anything
If it means that you see Jesus in me

Don't give up
Don't give up

Heal me and I shall be healed
Save me and I shall be saved

And my faith grows deeper
As my eyes see clearer
That you are my Healer and my God

Nearly ten years on and I'm standing with the nurses from Ward 27, alive and well.

Sarah and my sister Becki. Both were running the Race for Life. Not in memory of ... but in celebration of my healing.

—LIFE OUT LOUD GUIDE—

 THINK: OUT LOUD: What strikes you about what you have read?

How do you think gaining a good perspective can help? Do you have faith in the power of God for you? How do you think God uses a process to a help us? How can we be open to partnering with God and others?

 READ: OUT LOUD: Read again through the song lyrics — Healing is on its way.

PRAY: OUT LOUD: Father, thank you that you are a generous God and that your desire and will is to heal and make whole. I pray that you will help me to be open to the processes that can help me grow in you. May you gift me with the faith to believe in your power for my life today and to partner with you and others in seeing your kingdom come.

LIVE: OUT LOUD: Read through the healing check-list at the end of this chapter. Are there things here that you need to do? Or are there things you can help others with?

CHAPTER 11
PREPARATION TIME IS
NOT WASTED TIME

To live LIFE OUT LOUD we need to understand that preparation time is necessary for all of us. Although this can be a hard time, it is never a wasted time.

A great friend of mine once made this statement to me: preparation time is never wasted time. God is constantly preparing us for what He has prepared for us. Procrastination time is wasted time, but preparation time is not. This chapter is quite difficult to write because, more than anywhere else in this book, here I am preaching to myself.

A good way to explain this would be with a classic preacher example, full of wonderful analogy. Imagine you are a plane. I like to think of myself as an agile Stealth Bomber, but anyway... Planes are designed and created for one purpose: flight. Before the wheels of a plane can ever leave the ground, however, it goes through various stages of preparation to ensure that when the big moment comes the plane is ready and able to reach its full potential. Even when sat as a passenger on a plane this process can feel tedious and, in the busyness of life, a little unnecessary. But whether we like it or not, it is essential.

So the plane is parked at the gate, ready to depart, with its course and destination set. The instruments are checked; the plane is ready to move. Now something a little different has to happen. Even though the plane is equipped with many intelligent devices utilising cutting edge technology, it still requires help to get it moving. It is pushed backwards from the gate and re-positioned, ready for taxiing.

Similarly, we constantly need close guidance and help to start moving, even if we think we are capable of much more. We also need to learn that sometimes we may have to move backwards for a short while to enable a re-positioning for the right path. The next stage in our preparation time may be like taxiing. We feel like we are on the move, but the pace is slow. We may even look out of our metaphorical plane window to see other people further on in the journey. We may see some friends or colleagues already on the runway or, further still, we may see some in flight.

At this stage we may have the tendency to become a little bitter because we think we are ready. We believe this because we apply our own time constraints and sometimes forget that God knows perfect timing. We may even see people take off ahead of us who we feel don't deserve it or have not had to experience the same preparation time as us. It would be very easy to become judgmental. But preparation time is essential for a long and healthy flight. Without the proper preparation some people may not stay in the air as long as you do!

So, you're in line and ready for the next stage of the journey. Nobody likes to wait in line, but we all have to do it. The moment arrives and we are instructed to take our position on the runway. One final check takes place, but we can't go until we hear the word. In this example it's the audible voice of air traffic control, but many of us know that we don't often get the go-ahead by hearing the audible voice of God. We look for other signs. Is the runway clear? Do our instruments work? Is the weather right? Are there other people behind us in the line spurring us on to move? Is my crew on board ready?

If we can answer yes to all of these it may be a good indication that it is time to depart. The time has come. You've waited a long time for this moment. Make sure you give it all you have but remember to climb steadily to altitude. Most good things grow at a steady pace. You may experience turbulence on the way up, like an opposing force suggesting that you can't do this. Have a tough skin and ride it out. Eventually you will reach the required altitude and you will be flying.

What a process to go through just to get to this one point in time. You now need to remember that maintenance and progression on the journey is key. Don't fall into presumption – that now preparation time is over you can put on the autopilot and relax. Far from it. Constantly check the instruments, the weather, your position and your team to be on the front foot. There is no problem with switching on the autopilot now and again, but just remember one thing ... never leave the chair.

In the Bible we see many famous characters who also

experienced preparation time before walking into some of God's promises over their lives.

Joseph is the classic example of a man who had to wait a long time for the fulfilment of the promises over his life. At the age of 17 he was dreaming dreams and the sky was the limit, but within a short period of time it seemed as though he would never make it. He was misunderstood by his brothers, sold into slavery, wrongly accused of immorality and as an innocent man did a spell in prison. However, through all these adverse circumstances God was preparing a great leader who would one day literally save the world. Joseph was so convinced that God was with him in his unhappy journey that when he could have had revenge on his brothers he made this incredible confession: *"You intended to harm me, but God intended it for good to accomplish what is now being done, the saving of many lives."* (Genesis 50:20)

Moses had to overcome weaknesses of speech and wait longer for God's day because of his natural desire to make things happen. Though he was called to be a deliverer he had to wait for God's timing and find out that a personal agenda to kill an Egyptian perhaps meant more character building days in obscurity. However, the lesson is that his day eventually arrived.

Joshua needed to learn the ropes of leadership as a "number two" before he fully entered into his destiny. Days of preparation are never wasted. Timothy in the New Testament had to work through his weaknesses and fears. He learned the ministry through serving others. In today's church world, good character is so important. Pressures, hardships and delays can often be the tools God uses to shape us on the inside before much in the public arena can happen.

Then, of course, there is the greatest example of all who lived, Jesus. 30 years of obedience before embarking on three years of wonderful ministry fulfilling the Father's will.

Upon completing my treatment I walked into 2004 thinking I was ready to take on the world again. I had an incredible story to tell and some songs that everyone needed to hear. However, it's now 10 years on and I'm only just walking into some of my dreams. Although preparation time is a hard time, it is never wasted time.

A shot from the middle of the crowd for The Moment's debut live worship album. I dreamed of doing this and it became a reality.

—LIFE OUT LOUD GUIDE—

THINK: OUT LOUD: What strikes you about what you have read?

What times of preparation have you experienced? What God-given dreams and aspirations are inside you? How are you planning and preparing for these to come into reality?

READ: OUT LOUD: Genesis 50:19-21:
"But Joseph said to them, 'Don't be afraid. Am I in the place of God? You intended to harm me, but God intended it for good to accomplish what is now being done, the saving of many lives. So then, don't be afraid. I will provide for you and your children.' And he reassured them and spoke kindly to them."

PRAY: OUT LOUD: Father, thank you that you have called me and that you have specific plans and purposes for me. May I always be open to your preparation and work in my life. Help me to plan and prepare for all the things you have for me. May I never be on "auto-pilot" but ever learning and reaching for you. Amen.

LIVE: OUT LOUD: How could you serve someone else who has a similar dream or vision to you? In Joseph's life we see that he served other people's dreams first. Think about the things you are passionate about – who else is doing that around you? Serve them.

CHAPTER 12
FREEDOM CALLS MY NAME

When we choose to live LIFE OUT LOUD we have to learn how to manage our emotions, especially natural fears and anxieties. Is it possible to overcome all fears? Little by little...

Fear is a very unpleasant emotion that visits all of us from time to time. It is an unwelcome emotion, caused by the belief that someone or something may be in danger, a threat or a source of pain. Fear is often an overwhelming anxiety concerning possible outcomes. If I can be really honest with you, I would love to tell you that I don't experience these feelings or worry because I am now well. It's not quite as easy as that. I really do wish it was, but I am still a human being.

Fear comes knocking at my door most days. Some days the sound of the knocking is deafening. Some days the sound is a little fainter. I am constantly believing that as time passes the sound will begin to change and other sounds will dominate my thinking. I look to the day when God's soundtrack can be turned up and I can live life out loud in complete freedom. I still need to learn how to take my thoughts captive and bring them under the authority of God's word. I believe that one day I will be able to read news stories and see documentaries about illness without feeling uneasy or nervous. I believe that one day any abnormal aches and pains will not concern me and drag me into a spiral of worry. Unfortunately, being a Christian does not make us exempt from worldly emotions such as fear. So how do we manage it?

I have learnt that in some situations fear is just an emotion of the unknown. Often what we fear is in the future and hasn't actually happened yet. Some future situation may well warrant a natural fear because of its certainty, but we can control how we deal with this emotion in the time between now and then. The Bible says in Luke 12:

"Then Jesus said to his disciples: 'therefore I tell you, do not worry about your life, what you will eat; or about your body, what you will wear. Life is more than food, and the body more than clothes. Consider the ravens: They do not sow or reap, they have no storeroom or barn; yet God feeds them. And how much more valuable you are than birds! Who of you by worrying can add a single hour to his life? Since you cannot do this very little thing, why do you worry about the rest?"

We may read this verse and think "easier said than done". But wouldn't it be a great feeling if we did not have to worry about what tomorrow may bring. So much of our lives are wasted with unnecessary worry. It is proven that excessive worry will have a direct effect on our health, causing undesired symptoms which we really could do without. Here are a few of my ideas to help us manage our fears, so that we really can live in a town called Freedom! I created an acrostic that may help you. Take a look at this:

F fault

R rest

E exercise

E express

D direct

O overcome

M mind

FAULT: Fear, anxiety or worry can come through a personal conviction of sin or guilt. It may be something that happened in the past that has not been properly dealt with. Ask for forgiveness and set it right.

REST: According to the latest research our bodies need between 7-9 hours sleep per night in order to function at our fullest capacity. Lack of rest and lack of sleep cannot only lead to physical problems and ill health, but a direct increase in fears and anxiety. Make sure you have a good amount of sleep and rest!

EXERCISE: Medical studies show that exercise can help to reduce anxiety. Why not attempt a little exercise? Exercise not only reduces anxiety, it can also help to reduce stress. Get that old bike out of the garage or have a look for that lost pair of running shoes! Start with a simple walk.

EXPRESS: Never keep worries, fears or anxiety to yourself. Talk about them and share them with the right individuals. Start with a friend, meeting your small group leader or church pastor.

Some issues may come to light that require professional help or advice. Don't worry, this is not a bad thing, they are there for a reason!

DIRECT: We were never designed to be alone and we were not designed to deal with these issues alone. 1 Peter 5:7 tells us to cast all of our cares (meaning fears, worry and anxieties) onto Jesus because He in return cares for us. God gives us a target towards which we direct our cares. The target is God Himself.

OVERCOME: The only way to gain control of this is "little by little". In Exodus 23:28-29 we read a great illustration to help with this point. In order to possess the land God's people would have to move little by little. As their faith and strength increased, so would their territory. If they tried to do too much too quickly, the land and what it contained would be too great for them to handle. Be realistic, set short-term goals and you will overcome your fears. How quickly, you may ask? Little by little.

MIND: The battle ground usually designated for a fight against fear is your mind. The human mind is a very powerful thing and when it is allowed to wander it can sometimes be very difficult to bring back under control. According to some scientific research it is said that the human mind will process around 70,000 thoughts per day. I'm guessing that out of 70,000 there are going to be a few bad ones! That's natural. Let's choose to win every battle of the mind and the rest will follow.

To finish this chapter I have included the lyrics to a song that was written by Chris Eaton and me, called "Freedom Calls My Name". How fitting! My prayer for you is that you can experience this wonderful word called freedom in your own life. Our steps may be little by little, but just remember the famous fable of the hare and the tortoise. Those same little steps won the race.

Sin is no longer your master
It's time to serve one another
Remember not the former things
Consider them forgotten
I will do a new thing
Behold I will do a new thing

Freedom calls my name
Freedom calls my name
If the Son sets you free you shall be free indeed
Freedom calls my name

Everything is possible for you
Live your life free do not worry
Don't care for what tomorrow brings
Just go on spread your wings and fly
You know you were born to
Just fly, you know you were born to

Freedom calls my name
Freedom calls my name
If the Son sets you free, you shall be free indeed
Freedom calls my name

I cry Freedom, Freedom
Freedom calls my name
I cry Freedom, Freedom
Freedom calls my name

Me and my brothers. It's okay, you can laugh.

—LIFE OUT LOUD GUIDE—

THINK: OUT LOUD: What strikes you about what you have read?

Are you affected by fear? How did reading the FREEDOM acrostic help you? How could you begin to take small steps to win the race?

READ: OUT LOUD: Luke 12:
"Then Jesus said to his disciples: 'therefore I tell you, do not worry about your life, what you will eat; or about your body, what you will wear. Life is more than food, and the body more than clothes. Consider the ravens: They do not sow or reap, they have no storeroom or barn; yet God feeds them. And how much more valuable you are than birds! Who of you by worrying can add a single hour to his life? Since you cannot do this very little thing, why do you worry about the rest?"

PRAY: OUT LOUD: Father, I thank you that you love and care for me. I know that you are interested in my life and have given good things to me. I ask that I would be thankful for all that you have given me and done for me. Allow me to experience your peace and rest in all my life and to be free from worry. Freedom calls my name.

LIVE: OUT LOUD: Which areas of the FREEDOM acrostic could you work on this week?

CHAPTER 13
INVESTING IN LOCAL CHURCH

To live LIFE OUT LOUD we need to understand the importance of the local church and church attendance.

Most of us may have learnt in Sunday School the wonderful revelation that the church is the people not the building. I can remember our Sunday School teacher asking the class to draw the church. Of course, all of the children drew the building, which is understandable. The teacher then revealed that we were all wrong by unveiling his own illustration of the church which was, of course, a crowd of people.

I was a little sad at this point. Not just because I got the answer wrong, but also because I had spent a lot of time perfecting the church spire which was particularly difficult to draw.

My personal view, especially in this day and age, is that we sometimes get things out of perspective regarding the need for a church building or corporate gathering. I don't agree with the concept of meeting with a few friends at the local coffee house on a Sunday morning and calling it church. That can be done during the week. When Sunday morning arrives there should be just one thing on your mind: whatever it takes, I need to be in church today. Not out of compulsion or pressure, but out of a genuine desire to be with one another to worship God.

During my treatment I made the decision that church attendance was still a top priority, regardless of the natural circumstances. After coming out of hospital on a Thursday afternoon, after three gruelling days of chemotherapy, I would go straight to worship practice. If I was unable to stand, I would just sit on a chair and play my guitar. Throughout my treatment I never missed one worship practice or church service.

Hopefully you can see my passion for this wonderful gift called the local church. Attendance is important, but we also need to invest in this incredible gift – and by that I mean with actual money.

I'm definitely not the right person to give great theological insights into tithing, but I can give you my personal experience. I have tithed my money from a young age and continue to do so. I will until the day I die. This has proven to be the best investment I could possibly make with my finances. Better than a pension; better then a house, a car, stocks and shares; what I'm investing in is certain. Everything else will fade away. Investments can collapse, houses will eventually crumble, cars will die, but God's gift called the local church will last forever.

When my wife and I give our 10% each month we are doing one thing: saying thank you. Thank you to God for allowing me the opportunity to be part of this incredible thing called Life.

Thank you for your healing power. Thank you for my body. Thank you for this clean air that I breathe. Thank you for the family and friends that you have given me to love and be loved by. Thank you for food and drink on my table. Thank you for the roof over my head. Thank you for my church. Thank you for allowing me to be a father. Thank you for my sons. Thank you for my church. Thank you for the Bible. Thank you for the gift of music. Thank you for my God-given gifting and abilities. Thank you for my guitar. Thank you for life's beautiful backdrop, your creation. Thank you for life's adventures and opportunities...

I have all of this for just 10% of my income? What's even better is that this money is not even mine anyway – it is God's! I just have the challenge of stewarding it. You may say, "I can't even meet my bills, so how can I tithe?" Start with what you do have. Give your time, give your skills, give your passion. Then give financially as soon as you are able. We all have something we can give. There is no excuse to give nothing.

To put this in perspective, there are 168 hours in the week, 2 of which would be used to attend church. If my maths is correct this leaves us with 166 hours to do whatever we want. Out of 100% of our finances, God only asks for 10%, once again leaving a huge 90% for ourselves. There is no doubt about it, we serve a generous God.

I can remember one time walking through church at the end of a service to be greeted by a lady. At the time I was right in the middle of chemotherapy and looked a little worse for wear. She said to me, "How can you come to church when all of this is happening to you?" My reply was straight to the point and not politically correct. "Sorry if this offends," I replied, "but that is probably one of the most ridiculous questions I have ever been asked." She looked a little shocked. Then I said, "How could I *not* be in church when all of this is happening to me?"

To end this chapter I have included the lyrics to a song that was written by myself and Chris Eaton. It was written about my love for the local church, The City On A Hill. Enjoy!

V1
Out of the ashes
The Spirit moves
The walls are rebuilding
To bring good news
The church is arising
To stand up strong
The flame of revival
Is burning on

CH
City on a hill, shining for the world to see
City on a hill, God in all His Majesty
Bringing hope, Bringing peace, Bringing healing
Bringing love, Bringing life, Bringing freedom,
We are one, we belong, we believe in...
The city on a hill

V2
Power and Passion
The word of truth
The light in the darkness

Will guide us through
The church is arising
To stand up strong
The flame or revival
Is burning on

CH
City on a hill, shining for the world to see
City on a hill, God in all His Majesty
Bringing hope, Bringing peace, Bringing healing
Bringing Love, Bringing life, Bringing freedom,
We are one, we belong, we believe in...
The city on a hill

BRIDGE
Open wide the gates
Let the people come
They will find a place of holiness
Where all the pain is gone
Where every hand is held
Let the people come...

—LIFE OUT LOUD GUIDE—

 THINK: OUT LOUD: What strikes you about what you have read?

How has the local church impacted your life? How connected are you to your local church? Does this need to change?

 READ: OUT LOUD: Read through the lyrics of the song. Allow the words to stir in you a love for the church.

 PRAY: OUT LOUD: Father, I thank you for the wonderful idea of church. I ask that you would stir in me an increased passion for your people and for the power of gathering together each week. Help me to serve you with all my heart, soul and strength, in the powerful name of Jesus.

 LIVE: OUT LOUD: What one thing could you do this week to connect more strongly to your local church – do it!

CHAPTER 14
LEADING WHILE BLEEDING
(A PARENT'S PERSPECTIVE)
- STUART BELL

When we heard the news that David had cancer we entered a world we were not prepared for. I personally have never felt at home in hospitals and now suddenly we were confronted with little bald babies, feeding tubes and very poorly children.

Our world was challenged on every side. Would David lose his eye or worse, his life? What would be the implications for the next number of years with regard to family, relationships and particularly church ministry? We had never felt that by being in church leadership we were exempt from the pressures and problems of life, but now we were in the biggest battle of our lives. I knew that David needed to be my focus and realised that the time, energy, emotional strength and many miles of travel would have to be balanced with the demands of a relatively large church and a network of churches for which I was responsible. Irene and I decided that "bleeding in public" was not appropriate, but that vulnerability and weakness were important for our journey ahead.

We soon discovered the love of our church family as people responded to our needs. Both of us testify to a strange grace that seemed to be available to us that kept our heads above water. We certainly went through fire without being burned. These were some of the things that we learned on the way:

Firstly, we learned that we couldn't face the future on our own. Our starting point was to heavily lean on God. Having shared many sermons on "trusting God", "God's sovereign purposes in our lives" and "God's goodness and kindness" it was now time to practice what we had preached. We had to move from the theoretical to the practical. I remember having thought that life's difficulties can either make us bitter or better. It was now our turn to become better followers of Jesus. We had to stop feeling sorry for ourselves and put our trust in God, whatever the outcome.

I therefore made up my mind that I would not abdicate my responsibilities. I still continued with regular preaching and teaching and tried not to speak too often of our personal struggles, though on occasion our pain was evident. However, I did realise that there would be the possibility that my thinking would be more "maintenance" and "holding on" than vision and direction for the church. I therefore decided to invite a man known for his prophetic preaching to stand alongside me. So, for a two year period Duane and Kris White from Texas moved to Lincoln to help keep us on track. We will always remain grateful to those who stood with us in prayer and support.

The second thing we learned was that we must not face issues as professional leaders, but as ordinary Christian pilgrims. It was amazing to us that because of our position some would assume that we wouldn't feel the same pressures as so called "ordinary" believers, as though we were endued with extra-special ability and protection. The reality was, we were hurting badly. We were therefore grateful for those who, for a number of years, we had chosen to be accountable to. They provided strong support and love. On occasions they challenged us.

I remember one evening after I had shared in a leadership conference in South Africa, two of our closest friends took me to one side. They lovingly but firmly talked of how they had noticed that we had focused strongly on the work of God, but that we now needed to take some time out. They particularly advised Irene and I to take some holiday together as we needed quality time for ourselves. They outlined how pressure could build up on the inside and it was now appropriate to take a break. As we chatted further, I felt emotions rising up which eventually exploded into tears. It wasn't that I was particularly feeling anything at the time, but maybe it was because I felt safe enough to let the pressure out. It must be incredibly difficult for people who have no one to share their inner feelings with. As fellow believers it's great to be able to "weep with those who weep and rejoice with those who rejoice."

Thirdly, we came to understand more about the power of prayer and prophecy. I was deeply aware that as senior leaders Irene and I were being watched. We knew that we needed to be good examples of how people should face major issues of life. We knew that simply reciting scriptural truths or giving sound-bite clichés wasn't going to cut it. We desperately wanted to walk forward with integrity and needed personal faith and conviction.

This was when we began to highly value the prayers of our church family. A number of people were determined to be in for the long haul and regularly committed themselves to extended periods of both personal and corporate prayer. We were deeply grateful for the faith and tenacity of our Nigerian brothers and sisters within the church, who taught us all how to boldly stand on God's word and declare His will. It's remarkable how God spoke to us personally from scriptures that we had read many times before, but they came to us with fresh insight and understanding.

When David asked me perhaps the biggest question I've ever been asked, "Dad, am I going to die?" I didn't want to give an answer based just on my human thoughts. In fact, my first reply was, "I don't know David, but what I can promise you is that we are going to fight this thing with everything we have." There did come a time where I was convinced that God had spoken to me from His word and at that point I declared what I felt God had said over David's life. We can now look back a decade later and see what God has done and we are immensely thankful. During our journey there were numerous words of prophecy given by trusted people that lifted us up and gave us hope for the future.

As we look back it's amazing that with God's help we kept leading, our church continues to be blessed and David is walking into his destiny a healed person.

A lovely picture of my parents, Stu & Reno (Stuart & Irene). Dad always looks a little awkward in family photos and does that slightly strange glare – a similar glare to that of someone secretly plotting some kind of assassination. I do love my parents. They are incredible.

CHAPTER 15
HEALTHY RELATIONSHIPS

If we want to adopt this ethos of attempting to live our LIFE OUT LOUD, we can't do it alone.

We have been placed on this tiny planet to serve God, but He didn't create us to fly solo. We need God, but we also need people. I have to be careful when addressing this subject as we are all so diverse; no one situation is the same. My relational experiences may be the complete opposite to yours. Your relationship with your father or mother could be one of love and devotion, but equally it could be a living nightmare. The relationship of a child to one parent may be close and caring, but to the other distant and cold. The spectrum will be vast, but with caution I would like to share with you my thoughts.

Having faced life-changing issues I am very aware that healthy relationships are a major key to living life out loud. There is nothing worse than disunity and broken relationships. I would like to start by talking about parents. There are 41 verses in the Bible that teach us the importance of honouring our parents. A familiar example of this is found in Ephesians 6:1-3:

"Children, obey your parents in the Lord, for this is right. 'Honour your father and mother' (this is the first commandment with a promise), 'that it may go well with you and that you may live long in the land."

The relationship I have with my parents is very different as I see my parents as two of my best friends. As you know, Dad was even one of the best men at my wedding. I honour my parents because I love them, but also because Jesus tells me to. He makes a promise that if I choose to act in this way, in return I may have the opportunity to live a long and good life.

There is only one person on this planet that I will look to if I have some natural worries or fears about my future and that is my Dad. We often go to the gym, mainly to sit in the sauna and chat about life together. After a recent visit it gives me great joy to share a very funny moment with you.

It was fairly quiet at the gym and after a pretty extensive sauna session we were in the empty changing rooms ready to get changed – or so we thought. Picture the scene … well actually, maybe don't.

Despite running down the beach in my pants, I'm not the kind of guy who really feels the need to walk around a public changing room completely naked. There are plenty of people out there who do feel this urge and I find you all a little disturbing. However, this particular occasion was different.

At this point in time the towel that would usually be wrapped around my waist to cover the essentials had worked its way north and was now around my neck to allow minimal disruption when putting my briefs back on.

Just as I am attempting to pull up said briefs, Dad thinks it will be funny, upon exiting the changing rooms, to give me quite a forceful and loud slap on my left bare buttock. Dad thought we were alone at this point. However, this historic act was actually witnessed by a few people who appeared from the hidden side of the changing room just at the wrong time. Using my God-given wit, I decided to inject a little more humour into this situation by pretending that I did not know the man who slapped my bare buttock. A look of shock and panic filled the faces of the few men now present in the male changing room. I shouted after Dad, "Who are you"? At this point Dad realised my cunning intention and was now trying to flee the scene of the crime as fast as possible, before anyone got a cleared view of the alleged offender. Still in character, I stood there dramatically shaking my head from the shock that this old man has now caused me. The other guys stood there speechless as I walked out of the room.

This story has no real relevance to this chapter, but it is quite funny.

Your relationship with your parents may be great. If so, do everything you can to keep it that way. For some it may not be that simple. Your parents may no longer be with us and only you know how that relationship ended. Or, you may have not actually experienced a real father or mother figure in your life. I may never fully understand your situation or what your past memories look like, but I do know one thing. From this day on you can make a choice; a choice to say that your father in heaven is faultless. Where our earthly parents may fail, we have a Dad in heaven who will always come through on His promises. Our heavenly Father is the perfect model. Maybe we need to draw a line in the sand today, honouring our Heavenly Father, by choosing to forgive our earthly parents or asking to be forgiven. Let's honour our parents.

Next on the list is marriage. I don't think I'm too qualified to share on this in great detail, as many people reading this book will have been married a lot longer than me. Some may have even been married more years than I have been alive! I may be young and naïve, but allow me to share a few thoughts.

Growing up in a large church means that you interact with many different people and see a very wide spectrum of marriages. I see some of our more senior church attendees who really prove that marriage can be a lifelong adventure that becomes more loving each day. They give younger married couples a great example of this God-given gift. Thankfully, in my experience, these examples often outweigh the stories of broken relationships, but unfortunately there are still far too many marriages that do not run the full course.

I am extremely protective of my marriage and I want to do everything I can to ensure that the wedding vows we spoke don't merely become words on a page, but are upheld as unbreakable promises. I often notice that grace becomes abused in relational breakdowns, especially in marriages. The theology of God's grace becomes blurred, leading people to believe that grace is the get-out clause entitling stupid decisions to be made that can be devastating to marriages. Here is how I see grace. Grace is a safety net not a trampoline. Both a safety net and a trampoline look similar in appearance and both have parallel effects in springing people back to their feet. However, they are both designed with very different purposes. A trampoline is built for the intentional and a safety net is built for the accidental. Grace is always under you ready to catch the accidental. It is not a trampoline, so please don't keep bouncing on grace!

If there are problems in your marriage, make a decision today to start to repair it. It may not happen overnight. It may take time and tears. Our partner is one of the best long-term gifts we are given in this life. Choose today to live life out loud together.

Finally, if we want to live life out loud we have to choose the right people to walk with. People we call friends. It is so important to surround yourself with good people. Individuals that are for you and believe the best for you. The kind of people who still speak the same of you when their door is open and when it is closed. Remember, you don't need to be present to receive praise. Proverbs 13:20 says, "Walk with the wise and become wise, for a companion of fools suffers harm." The Message translation puts it this way: "Become wise by walking with the wise; hang out with fools and watch your life fall to pieces." Sometimes, overly super-spiritual people can be as bad as an unbelieving friend. Mathew 16:6 says, "'Be careful,' Jesus said to them. 'Be on your guard against the yeast of the Pharisees and Sadducees.'" Who you connect with really matters in life. They will either lift you up or pull you down.

I end this chapter with a great quote from CS Lewis: "Is any pleasure on earth as great as a circle of Christian friends by a good fire?"

Thank God for family.

—LIFE OUT LOUD GUIDE—

 THINK: OUT LOUD: What strikes you about what you have read?

How have good friendships helped you in your life? Who can you get alongside to help in their journey of faith? Are there ways you could invest in your relationship with your parents and friends? If you are married, what positive step could you take to invest in and protect your marriage?

 READ: OUT LOUD: Proverbs 13:20 NIV:
"Walk with the wise and become wise, for a companion of fools suffers harm."

 PRAY: OUT LOUD: Father, I thank you for the good relationships around me. Help me to honour those around me and in doing so, to love you. I thank you that you are my Heavenly Father and that you are generous and loving towards me. May I invest well in good friendships and wise companions.

 LIVE: OUT LOUD: What good friendships or relationships are you inspired to invest in?

CHAPTER 16
LONGING FOR MONDAY
MORNINGS

So this is the final chapter of your guide to living life out loud. I really do hope that you have found it helpful. Once again, thank you so much for reading this book, it really does mean so much to me. It's a little difficult to try and end a book like this, as this really is a story that just keeps on growing. We started this book with my birth. The incredible news is, we don't end the book with the opposite. Far from it. We will end this book with a very exciting chapter. Here we go!

Longing for Monday mornings? A bit of a strange title. This is maybe because Monday mornings usually have a bad press across the globe.

They are certainly not usually "longed for". I did a little research into why this particular day of the week is the day that everyone dislikes and the two main answers were as follows:

Firstly, it is the furthest day away from the next weekend. Secondly it is the first day after the previous weekend. It appears to me that there is something very special about the weekend. That got me thinking as to why the weekend has become a focal point for so many people and why the 7 days in our week should contain such a contrast between good and bad. It's all down to one word. Perspective.

When thinking about this more I realised that all the days in our week are actually exactly the same. They just have different names. No one day is longer or shorter than another. No one day guarantees nicer weather. No one day always presents the best opportunities. I do know that the weekend is often associated more with recreation than work, but wouldn't it be incredible to have that same Friday feeling first thing on a Monday morning? Is that possible? Well, yes it is and that is what this book is all about.

Once I had caught the true revelation of how incredible this gift called life really is, my whole outlook changed. I really do enjoy every day, but if I had to pick a favourite time of the week it would honestly be Monday morning. Every time Monday morning comes around I open both eyes, take in a breath and I remember God's goodness to me. The week I am about to enter has endless opportunities and new experiences waiting, where anything really is possible ... anything.

I can remember going out for a meal with all of the family about three months after I had finished my treatment. There was nothing special about where we went and It wasn't even a special occasion. It was just a normal night where the family had got together. We all sat around a large table chatting about life and what we had all done in the last week. I held little Jermac on my knee and began to look around. That's when it hit me. I started to imagine that I was staring into a family photo of this very occasion, only to notice that I was not in the picture. I mentally zoomed out from the image to see if I was the one taking the picture ... but it was not me. At this moment I realised what this instant in time could have looked like. I held onto Jermac and started to cry with uncontainable tears. Everyone turned to see if I was okay. I tried to explain, as much as I could, what I was feeling and how there was nothing wrong with me, but I was just so happy to be alive. Life seemed so precious and I didn't want to miss a second of it.

It was a few months after this when I started to notice bigger changes in me. New perspectives towards life were coming to the surface. Sarah and I went to Spain to visit her grandparents. We stayed in a villa on the side of a mountain overlooking a large lake. When it comes to vacations I'm not usually the guy who likes to sit in a chair and read a book – unless it has lots of pictures in it. That's far too "grown up". I'm the guy that would be perfecting the art of the cannon ball into the swimming pool, just within splashing distance of those sat in chairs reading books without pictures. However, this time was different. I found myself sat on the balcony in a chair very quiet and very still, simply gazing at the view before me. I sat there for hours without moving or speaking, just looking at the mountains and all of the wildlife. I was captivated by creation.

This was not like me, it was quite unusual behaviour. Then it hit me. My perspective on this part of life had changed. Maybe before my health battle I had been too busy to notice the real beauty that can be seen through the human eye. I had the time here to take a closer look. I suppose with the possibility of losing my eyesight made me particularly thankful to be able to see all of this with two eyes. Another angle of life became more apparent to me and I wanted to find more angles that I had not yet seen. I was so thankful to be alive.

However, I couldn't stay this calm and sentimental for too long, so I decided to send a post card to Mum and Dad stating that I had joined the Foreign Legion, got a tattoo on my face and was currently writing from a Spanish prison where I was sharing a cell with my new little Spanish friend, Carlos.

Let's bring this incredible journey a little closer to the present day. A few months after completing my treatment I attended Music College and enrolled on the session musician course. You will be very pleased to know that I passed the course with a distinction! Knowing that a fulltime profession in the music industry straight away may be a little far fetched, a good friend of the family offered me a job in a large construction company as a trainee contracts manager. Quite different from playing guitar, but I was very aware that life still carries on around us and the bills still needed paying. This job allowed me to get a mortgage and furnish our new house. This was an ideal career path for someone, but I don't think it was for me.

Throughout my life I have always had the streak of an entrepreneur running through me. So just two weeks before I got married I decided to leave a secure and well-paid job and start in business. Classic Dave. My ventures have ranged from event management through to setting up an American hotdog franchise. A good friend once told me that a dream without action is merely a fantasy, so I made the decision to take action upon my dreams. My aim was to have a business income that could help support my dream to be involved in worship and music. It's great to have the vision, but you still need the provision to make it happen.

I have had the pleasure of being involved in many bands over the years and have had some great opportunities to work alongside some great musicians. So when I heard that the song writing legend, Chris Eaton, was coming to our home church to do a special concert I did everything I could to be there. At the end of the night I rushed over to speak to Chris and his wife Abby. I had the opportunity to share a little of my journey and how I was involved in music. It was at this point that I knew this couple was of a different order – simply because they had the time to listen and took a genuine interest in me. When you reach a certain level people can have the ability to just smile at enthusiastic faces, but not pay any attention. But this was not the case. Email addresses were exchanged which later resulted in an invitation to their house to spend a few days song writing. To date, we have written many songs together, both worship and secular. Sarah and I count them both as close friends.

As you will see, throughout my life music is something I have always held on to and never given up on. Other Ideas and fascinations may have come and gone until now, but what is really in your heart is often revealed when it is still on your to-do list 10 years down the line. With this is mind I wanted to launch a brand new worship band that would be able to use the original songs written by Chris and myself, but also to act as a vehicle to allow me to share my story of hope. The dream was a little bigger than "just another band" on the scene.

I believe that God allowed me to dream in greater measure about this. I had visions of crowds of people having an encounter with the living God through worship. I had visions of people rushing the sick to one of our concerts because through our praying and playing miracles would be manifest. I saw people arrive in wheelchairs and leave the venue running. I saw hundreds accepting Jesus as their Lord and Saviour for the very first time.

I believe that if your vision does not scare you, then it's not big enough and this one certainly scares me a little. To play my part in making this a reality I formed the worship band called The Moment. We decided to call it that because we believe everyone has a "moment". There are God-moments waiting for everyone. Jesus is passing by, it is our mandate to help people not to miss their moment – whether that is a moment in worship, a moment of finding salvation or a moment of receiving healing.

When forming the band the biggest challenge was finding the right people. Musicians are a very interesting breed and it is not common to find someone who has the two key attributes that are essential to something like this: capability and character. I have noticed that it is quite easy to find someone who is extremely capable in their individual gifting, but it can often mean that character issues are sacrificed.

On the reverse, it is also easy to find someone who walks with integrity and is on the same song sheet spiritually, but may not be as capable as his or her peers. Character is by far the more important of the two attributes, but to find someone who is capable with the character to match is uncommon.

However, God brought a few individuals across my path that were not only incredibly gifted, but also the real deal on the platform. They prioritised local church, were using their gifting purely for the glory of God and also shared a very similar vision to myself. They were a God-given gift to me, which formed The Moment. During our first 18 months of being a band we had travelled to the USA twice and had the opportunity to play in some incredible churches. We had seen around 600 first time commitments to follow Christ and some incredible and real healing testimonies outworked through our ministry.

On Friday February 1, 2013 we recorded our debut live worship album, Freedom Calls. I was quite nervous about putting on a big concert with us guys as the only attraction. I had visions of walking out on stage to find that the only people in the auditorium were my Mum and Dad! Thankfully this was not a prophecy. We walked out onto the stage to see that just under 900 people had turned up to worship with us. What an incredible night and a great launch for this amazing thing called The Moment. I believe that God's plans for this are big. I'm very excited to see it all unfold with great friends around me.

We are nearly up to date with the journey so far. I am currently 26 years old and life has never been better. After all that God has done for me I want to spend the rest of my days here on planet earth attempting to pay Him back. It will be a losing battle from day one as this will never be possible in my lifetime. What Jesus has done for me is too much to ever repay. However, I can still make an attempt. By this I mean every morning committing my life to Him, offering to serve Him in any way possible. It may be on a stage with thousands of people hearing my story and singing our songs, or it might just be me being the best father and husband I can possibly be. I want to make the most of every opportunity I have.

Life is a gift and I am so thankful for my change of perspective. This newfound way of thinking has now shaped the course of my life. I really annoy Sarah at times, as I never want to go to sleep at night. Don't get me wrong, as a married couple an early night can have one or two advantages, if you know what I mean ... but I stay awake late at night because If I'm asleep I will be missing out on life!

To mark the 10-year anniversary of complete health, Sarah and I took all of the family away to a big theme park. We all stayed in a hotel the night before and then went into the park the next day. It was raining when we arrived, which appeared to have an effect on the people waiting to get inside, who all looked a little miserable. But for us, the rain just made us celebrate more. It was a day of fun and laughter with family and to honour a wonderful thing called life. I will remember this day for many years to come.

I believe that it is God's will that I continue to live a healthy, but also a long life. I have claimed verse 16 of psalm 91: *"With long life I will satisfy him and show him my salvation."* I truly believe that Sarah and I will grow very old together and what is in the past remains in the past. I will be around to see all my children grow up and have families of their own. I will be there on their graduation days and wedding days. I will experience all the joys of being a grandfather. I will own a bus pass and draw a pension. Actually, a little more specifically, I will own a bus and draw a pension from all my growing investments!

In closing, I see myself as an old man answering the same questions stated in the introduction to this book. Lying very peacefully with my family all around me, children and grandchildren looking back at my life, just moments away from seeing my Maker face to face. Knowing what I would say in this divine moment is easy. It has been planned since December 2003 when I was just 16 years of age. There will be no questioning, no why's, no regrets, no if only's ... I will simply say, "Lord, thank you for being so good to me. What a wonderful life it has been."

Thank you for reading this book. If in many years down the line you come looking for me, I will still be living Life Out Loud.

—LIFE OUT LOUD GUIDE—

 THINK: OUT LOUD: What strikes you about what you have read?

Think through all that you have read and learned. What stands out most? Where have you been most challenged in your life? Who is on that journey with you? What are you going to do now?

 READ: OUT LOUD: John 10:10 NIV:
"I have come that they may have life, and have it to the full."

 PRAY: OUT LOUD: Father, I ask that you would help to me see my life from a different perspective today. Help me to follow you and the plans you have for me. May I live well each day knowing it is a gift from you and may my life be full of gratitude and faith. I want to live life – OUT LOUD!

LIVE: OUT LOUD: LIVE LIFE OUT LOUD!

A few glimpses into our world right up to the present day. My beautiful wife. My miracle boys. My passion for music. What a wonderful life.

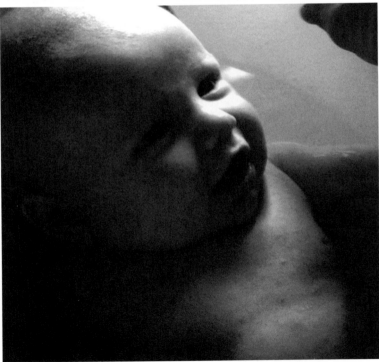

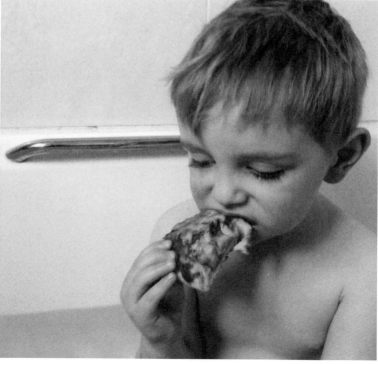

Paul Blundel, Rick Warren and Yours Truly